Gooseberry Patch co.®

One-Pot Meals

Flavor without the fuss...home-cooked
dinners your family will love!

Gooseberry Patch
2500 Farmers Dr., #110
Columbus, OH 43235

www.gooseberrypatch.com

1·800·854·6673

Copyright 2005, Gooseberry Patch 978-1-62093-117-2
First Printing, March, 2013

Photo Edition is a major revision of *One-Pot Meals*.

Check out our cooking videos on YouTube!

Scan this code with your smartphone or tablet...it takes you
right to our YouTube playlist of cooking videos for **One-Pot
Meals**. While there, you can also view our entire collection
of **Gooseberry Patch** cooking videos!

If you spot this icon next to a recipe name, it means we
created a video for it. You'll find it at **www.youtube.com/
gooseberrypatchcom**.

Contents

Dedication

Dedicated to all of our friends who love
a home filled with inviting aromas and
cozy comforts as much as we do!

Appreciation

A hearty thanks to all of you who
shared your tastiest
one-pot recipes with us!

Home on the Range

STOCKPOT, SKILLET & PRESSURE-COOKER MEALS

My Favorite One-Pot Meal

Liz Plotnick-Snay
Gooseberry Patch

Curry powder, raisins and chopped apple make this chicken dish just a little different.

2 onions, diced
1/4 c. oil, divided
2-1/2 to 3 lbs. boneless, skinless chicken breasts
14-1/2 oz. can diced tomatoes
1/2 c. white wine or chicken broth
1 T. curry powder
1/4 t. garlic powder
1/4 t. dried thyme
1/4 t. nutmeg
1 apple, cored, peeled and cubed
1/4 c. raisins
3 T. whipping cream
1/2 t. lemon juice
2 c. prepared rice

Sauté onions in 2 tablespoons oil over medium heat in a large skillet; remove onions and set aside. Add remaining oil and chicken to skillet; heat chicken until golden. Return onions to skillet; add tomatoes, wine or broth and spices. Mix well; reduce heat, cover and simmer for 20 minutes. Add apple, raisins and cream; simmer over low heat for an additional 6 to 8 minutes. Stir in lemon juice. Serve over prepared rice. Makes 3 to 4 servings.

There's no need to be formal with one-pot meals...set the pot in the center of the dinner table and let everyone help themselves!

Deep South Chicken & Dumplings ▶ *Christian Brown*
Killeen, TX

One of those comfort foods that everybody loves! It's extra special made with homemade broth, but if you're short on time, a good canned broth is fine.

3 to 4-lb. roasting chicken   Garnish: fresh parsley
salt and pepper to taste

Roast chicken, covered, in an ungreased roasting pan at 350 degrees for 1-1/2 hours. Let chicken cool while preparing Supreme Sauce. Shred chicken; add to simmering sauce. Drop Dumplings into sauce by heaping tablespoonfuls. Cover and cook over high heat 10 to 15 minutes, or until dumplings are firm and puffy. Discard bay leaves. Add salt and pepper; garnish with fresh parsley. Serves 6.

Supreme Sauce:

2 T. butter   2 bay leaves
1 T. oil   5 T. all-purpose flour
1/2 c. carrots, peeled and diced 6 c. chicken broth
1/2 c. celery, diced   1/4 c. whipping cream
3 cloves garlic, minced

Melt butter and oil in a Dutch oven over medium heat. Add vegetables, garlic and bay leaves. Sauté until soft. Stir in flour; add broth, one cup at a time, stirring well after each addition. Simmer until thickened; stir in cream.

Dumplings:

2 c. all-purpose flour   2 eggs
1 T. baking powder   3/4 to 1 c. buttermilk, divided
1 t. salt

Mix flour, baking powder and salt. Whisk together eggs and 3/4 cup buttermilk; fold into flour mixture. Stir just until dough forms, adding a little more buttermilk if needed.

Easy Bacon Frittata ▶️

Beth Bundy
Long Prairie, MN

Delicious and oh-so simple to put together! Pair with fruit salad
for brunch or a crisp green salad for an easy dinner.

3 T. oil
2 c. frozen shredded
   hashbrowns
7 eggs, beaten

2 T. milk
12 slices bacon, crisply cooked
   and crumbled
3/4 c. shredded Cheddar cheese

Heat oil in a large skillet over medium heat. Add hashbrowns and
cook for 10 to 15 minutes, stirring often, until golden. In a bowl,
whisk together eggs and milk. Pour egg mixture over hashbrowns in
skillet; sprinkle with bacon. Cover and reduce heat to low. Cook for
10 minutes, or until eggs are set. Sprinkle with cheese; remove from
heat, cover, and let stand about 5 minutes, until cheese is melted.
Cut into wedges to serve. Makes 6 servings.

Little touches at your main entrance will make
your family's days stress-free...coat hooks low enough
for kids to reach, a small basket for house keys and
a message board for daily reminders.

Orange-Pork Stir-Fry

Amy Butcher
Columbus, GA

Short on time? Pick up a package of pork that's precut in strips for stir-frying.

1-oz. pkg. Italian salad
    dressing mix
1/4 c. orange juice
1/4 c. oil
2 T. soy sauce

1 lb. pork loin, cut into strips
16-oz. pkg. frozen Oriental
    vegetable blend, thawed
2-1/2 c. prepared rice

Mix together dressing mix, juice, oil and soy sauce. Combine one tablespoon of dressing mixture and pork strips in a large skillet over medium heat. Heat and stir for 4 to 5 minutes or until meat is no longer pink. Add vegetables and remaining dressing mixture; heat and stir until vegetables are crisp-tender. Serve over prepared rice. Makes 4 servings.

Look for inexpensive Asian-themed plates, bowls and teacups at an import store. They'll make even the simplest Oriental meals special. Don't forget the fortune cookies!

Chicken Spaghetti

Glenna Martin
Uwchland, PA

An old family favorite!

1 lb. boneless, skinless chicken
   breasts, cut into bite-size
   pieces
1/4 to 1/2 c. butter
1 onion, chopped
8-oz. can sliced mushrooms,
   drained

16-oz. pkg. broccoli flowerets
1 clove garlic, minced
salt and pepper to taste
16-oz. pkg. spaghetti, cooked
Garnish: grated Parmesan
   cheese

In a large skillet, sauté chicken in butter until no longer pink. Add onion, mushrooms, broccoli and garlic; sauté until chicken is cooked through and vegetables are tender. Add salt and pepper to taste; toss with cooked spaghetti. Sprinkle with Parmesan cheese. Serves 4.

Mismatched glass salt & pepper shakers make sweet mini vases for the dinner table...pick up a few extras at yard sales. Simply remove the tops, fill with water and tuck in a big blossom. Place one at each table setting for a colorful accent.

Chicken-Pepper Pasta

Pamela Chorney
Providence Forge, VA

My husband and I love this dish. The aroma is wonderful!

6 T. margarine
1 onion, chopped
1 red pepper, chopped
1 yellow pepper, chopped
1 orange pepper, chopped
1 t. garlic, minced
3 lbs. boneless, skinless chicken
   breasts, cut into strips

1 T. fresh tarragon, minced
3/4 t. salt
1/4 t. pepper
3/4 c. half-and-half
1 c. shredded mozzarella cheese
1/2 c. grated Parmesan cheese
7-oz. pkg. vermicelli, cooked

In a skillet, melt margarine until sizzling; stir in onion, peppers and garlic. Cook over medium-high heat until peppers are crisp-tender, 2 to 3 minutes. Remove vegetables from skillet with a slotted spoon and set aside. Add chicken, tarragon, salt and pepper to skillet. Continue cooking, stirring occasionally, until chicken is golden and tender, 7 to 9 minutes. Add vegetables, half-and-half and cheeses to chicken mixture. Reduce heat to medium; continue heating until cheese has melted, 3 to 5 minutes. Add vermicelli; toss gently to coat. Serve immediately. Serves 4 to 6.

Over dinner, ask your children to tell you about books they're reading at school and return the favor by sharing books you loved as a child. You may find you have some favorites in common!

Skillet Macaroni & Beef

Lou Miller
Savannah, MO

*This is my favorite recipe...I usually have all the ingredients
on hand and my guests always love its hearty flavor.*

1-1/2 lbs. ground beef
2 c. elbow macaroni, uncooked
1/2 c. onion, minced
1/2 c. green pepper, chopped
2 8-oz. cans tomato sauce

1 c. water
1 T. Worcestershire sauce
1 t. salt
1/4 t. pepper

Lightly brown beef in a skillet; drain. Stir in macaroni, onion and
green pepper; heat until onion is soft. Add remaining ingredients.
Lower heat; cover and simmer 25 minutes or until macaroni is tender,
stirring occasionally. Serves 6 to 8.

A country-style wreath on your front door says "Welcome!"
to family & friends. Use a glue gun to decorate a grapevine
wreath with mini sunflowers and tie on a big
yellow raffia bow...charming!

One-Pot Spaghetti

Flo Burtnett
Gage, OK

Mmm good...spaghetti from scratch, and no need to use all the pans in the kitchen. My grandson Clay eats it up!

1 lb. ground beef
1 onion, diced
2 14-oz. cans chicken broth
6-oz. can tomato paste
1/2 t. dried oregano
1/2 t. salt
1/4 t. pepper
1/8 t. garlic powder
8-oz. pkg. spaghetti, uncooked
  and broken
Garnish: grated Parmesan
  cheese

Brown ground beef and onion in a large skillet over medium heat. Drain; return to skillet. Stir in broth, tomato paste and seasonings; bring to a boil. Add spaghetti; reduce heat and simmer, stirring often, 15 minutes or until spaghetti is tender. Sprinkle with cheese. Makes 4 servings.

While dinner simmers, pop some Parmesan bread in the oven. Split an Italian loaf lengthwise and place on a broiler pan. Spread with a mixture of 1/4 cup butter, 2 tablespoons grated Parmesan cheese, 2 teaspoons minced garlic and 1/4 teaspoon oregano. Broil until golden...scrumptious!

Shrimp Creole

Kathy Grashoff
Fort Wayne, IN

If your family likes Spanish Rice, they'll love this delicious seafood variation.

1 c. onion, chopped
1 c. green pepper, chopped
1 c. celery, sliced
2 cloves garlic, minced
1/4 c. butter
1/4 c. all-purpose flour
1 t. salt

pepper to taste
1 bay leaf
16-oz. can diced tomatoes
1-1/2 lbs. shrimp, peeled
   and cleaned
3 to 4 c. prepared rice

Sauté onion, green pepper, celery and garlic in butter in a skillet over medium heat until tender. Blend in flour; stir until golden. Add salt, pepper and bay leaf; stir in tomatoes until thick. Reduce heat to low; add shrimp and simmer, covered, for 10 minutes until shrimp are just pink, stirring occasionally. Discard bay leaf; serve over prepared rice. Serves 6 to 8.

Cloth napkins are so much nicer than paper ones!
Make napkin rings of grapevine and hot glue a different
button or charm on each.

Dad's Cajun Dinner

Kristen Blanton
Big Bear City, CA

Add more Cajun seasoning and hot pepper sauce if you dare!

1 onion, diced
1 t. garlic, minced
2 T. butter
2 green peppers, diced
5 stalks celery, diced
3 T. Cajun seasoning
14-oz. pkg. Kielbasa, sliced

15-oz. can kidney beans,
  drained and rinsed
14-1/2 oz. can diced tomatoes
12-oz. can tomato juice
hot pepper sauce to taste
3 c. prepared rice

Sauté onion and garlic in butter until onion is crisp-tender. Add peppers, celery and seasoning; continue to sauté until vegetables are tender. Add Kielbasa; sauté an additional 3 to 4 minutes. Add beans, tomatoes and tomato juice; cook until heated through. Sprinkle with hot sauce to taste. Serve over prepared rice. Makes 6 servings.

Serve your family dinner in an unexpected place, just for fun...a blanket in the backyard, a spread in the living room or even on the front porch. It's quick & easy with a one-pot meal and a delightful change from routine!

Home on the Range

Salsa Ranch Skillet

Mandi Smith
Delaware, OH

I created this delicious recipe for competition in the Ohio State Fair. It's very tasty, quick and easy to make.

1 lb. ground beef
1/2 c. sweet onion, chopped
1/2 c. green pepper, chopped
2.8-oz. pkg. ranch salad
    dressing mix
1 c. water
15-oz. can tomato sauce

16-oz. jar mild salsa
16-oz. can baked beans
8-oz. pkg. rotini pasta,
    uncooked
1 c. shredded Colby & Monterey
    Jack cheese

Brown ground beef with onion and green pepper in a large skillet over high heat. Stir in dressing mix until thoroughly blended. Stir in water, tomato sauce, salsa and beans; bring to a boil. Add pasta; reduce to medium-low heat. Simmer for 12 to 15 minutes until pasta is tender, stirring occasionally. Remove from heat; sprinkle with cheese and let stand for 5 minutes until cheese melts and sauce thickens. Serves 4 to 6.

Make the most of your front porch! A porch swing, rocking chairs, comfy pillows and hanging flower baskets create a cozy place for family & friends to visit and enjoy the fresh air.

Spicy Taco Salad

Allene Whalen
Salinas, CA

For a party presentation, arrange tortilla chips on a platter and top with ground beef and vegetables arranged in rings. Spoon the avocado sauce mixture over all.

1 lb. ground beef
1 head lettuce, shredded
15-1/2 oz. can kidney beans,
    drained and rinsed
6-oz. can sliced black olives,
    drained
3 tomatoes, sliced
4 green onions, chopped
1 c. shredded Monterey Jack
    cheese

2 avocados, mashed
1/4 c. oil
1 c. sour cream
1 T. chili powder
2 T. lemon juice
1 T. sugar
salt to taste
1/8 t. hot pepper sauce
10-oz. pkg. tortilla chips

Heat ground beef in a skillet until browned; drain and let cool. Toss together beef, lettuce, beans, olives, tomatoes, onions and cheese; set aside. Combine remaining ingredients except tortilla chips; toss with ground beef mixture. Add chips; toss lightly and serve immediately. Serves 4.

Serve Spicy Taco Salad in tortilla bowls! Lightly brush corn tortillas on both sides with olive oil. Carefully press into oven-safe soup bowls, folding up the edges. Bake at 325 degrees for 8 to 10 minutes, until crispy and golden.

Jo Ann's Garden Frittata ▶

Jo Ann

Family & friends are sure to love this savory egg dish. It's filled with brightly colored vegetables...beautiful to look at and delicious to eat.

4 thick slices bacon, chopped
1 onion, diced
1 red pepper, thinly sliced
1 c. corn
1 c. green beans, thinly sliced
1 bunch Swiss chard, thinly
   sliced

3 eggs, beaten
1-1/4 c. half-and-half
1/8 t. dried thyme
salt and pepper to taste
1 c. shredded Cheddar cheese

In a large oven-proof skillet over medium-high heat, cook bacon until crisp. Drain bacon on paper towels; reserve drippings. In one tablespoon drippings, sauté onion, red pepper and corn for 5 minutes. Add beans; sauté another 3 minutes. Transfer vegetable mixture to a bowl; set aside. Add one teaspoon drippings to skillet; sauté chard for 2 minutes. Add to vegetable mixture in bowl. In a separate large bowl, whisk eggs, half-and-half and seasonings. Stir in bacon, cheese and vegetable mixture; pour into skillet. Bake at 375 degrees for about 35 minutes, until set and crust is golden. Let stand for 10 minutes; cut into wedges. Makes 8 servings.

Laughter is the best dinnertime music.

-Carleton Kendrick

Herbed Mashed Potatoes

Vickie

*Filled with fresh herbs, these potatoes are just wonderful!
Serve topped with a large melting pat of butter, of course.*

6-1/2 c. potatoes, peeled and
   cubed
2 cloves garlic, halved
1/2 c. milk
1/2 c. sour cream
1 T. butter, softened

2 T. fresh parsley, minced
2 T. fresh oregano, minced
1 T. fresh thyme, minced
3/4 t. salt
1/8 t. pepper

Place potatoes and garlic in a large saucepan; add water to cover.
Bring to a boil over medium-high heat. Reduce heat to medium;
simmer for 20 minutes, or until potatoes are very tender. Drain; return
potatoes and garlic to pan. Add remaining ingredients; beat with an
electric mixer on medium speed to desired consistency. Serves 6 to 8.

Make herbed butter in a jiffy to dress up mashed potatoes
or serve with warm rolls. Simply roll a stick of butter
in freshly chopped herbs, slice and serve.

Smoky Sausage Stew

Marlene Darnell
Newport Beach, CA

Add a little hot pepper sauce if you like.

14-1/2 oz. can beef broth, divided
14-1/2 oz. can stewed tomatoes
16-oz. pkg. smoked bratwurst, sliced

4 new potatoes, cubed
2 onions, coarsely chopped
1 c. baby carrots
1/4 c. all-purpose flour
1 green pepper, diced

Set aside 1/4 cup beef broth. Combine remaining beef broth, tomatoes, bratwurst, potatoes, onions and carrots in a large stockpot over medium heat. Bring to a boil; reduce heat and simmer for 15 to 20 minutes until vegetables are tender. Combine reserved broth with flour, stirring until smooth; stir into pot until thickened. Add green pepper; simmer 3 minutes. Serves 6.

Mix & match different colors and patterns of place settings, just for fun!

Chilly Weather Chili

Mary Jo Babiarz
Spring Grove, IL

Garnish with Cheddar cheese stars that have been cut out with cookie cutters.

1 lb. ground beef
2 T. onion, diced
15-3/4 oz. can chili beans with
   chili sauce

8-1/4 oz. can refried beans
8-oz. can tomato sauce
8-oz. jar salsa
1/2 c. water

Brown beef and onion together in a large stockpot; drain. Add remaining ingredients. Bring to a boil and reduce heat to medium; cover and simmer for 30 minutes, stirring occasionally. Serves 4.

Make a cozy, quick & easy fleece throw for your sofa. Buy
a 2-yard length of colorful fleece and cut 6-inch fringes
along each edge...ready for snuggling!

Marvelous Minestrone

Barbara Bowen
Lewiston, ID

This hearty veggie-filled soup takes awhile to simmer, but it's so simple to toss together that you won't mind at all. It freezes well, so why not make a double batch?

1/4 c. olive oil
2 cloves garlic, chopped
1 c. onion, chopped
5 stalks celery, chopped
6 c. beef broth
2 6-oz. cans tomato paste
2 carrots, peeled and diced
2 leeks, chopped

2 c. cabbage, chopped
2 to 3 potatoes, peeled and diced
1 t. dried rosemary
salt and pepper to taste
15-1/2 oz. can kidney beans
3/4 c. elbow macaroni, uncooked
Garnish: grated Parmesan
   cheese

Heat oil in a large pot over medium heat; sauté garlic, onion and celery until tender. Stir in remaining ingredients except beans, macaroni and garnish. Bring to a boil; reduce heat to low. Cover and simmer for one hour, stirring occasionally. Stir in undrained beans and uncooked macaroni. Simmer, uncovered, for another 30 minutes, stirring occasionally, until macaroni is tender. Serve sprinkled with Parmesan cheese. Makes 8 to 10 servings.

Rediscover the fun of making colorful potholders. The little looms and weaving loops can still be purchased at craft stores. It's just as much fun as it was when you were a child, and you can always use more potholders!

Corned Beef & Cabbage

Heidi McInnish
Chula Vista, CA

A St. Patrick's Day tradition...but much too delicious to enjoy only once a year!

2 to 3 onions, chopped
1-1/4 lb. baby carrots
3-lb. corned beef brisket with
   seasoning packet
1/2 c. malt vinegar
Optional: 1/4 c. Irish stout

1-1/4 lbs. redskin potatoes
1 to 1-1/2 heads cabbage, cut
   into serving-size wedges
Garnish: coarse grain mustard,
   Dijon mustard

Arrange onions, carrots, corned beef and any liquid, seasoning packet, vinegar and stout, if desired, in a large stockpot. Add water just to cover the beef. Cover pot; bring to a boil. Reduce heat and simmer for 2-1/2 to 3 hours until meat is tender. Add potatoes and cabbage to pot. Cover and simmer over high heat 8 to 10 minutes; reduce to medium and simmer an additional 15 to 20 minutes until potatoes and cabbage are tender. Remove vegetables to serving dish; place corned beef on a cutting board. Let rest 2 to 3 minutes; remove any fat and slice across the grain. Serve with vegetables and mustards.
Serves 6 to 8.

Love cabbage...don't love the aroma? Use an old-fashioned trick to keep your house sweet-smelling. Just add a spoonful of vinegar, a lemon wedge or half an apple to the cooking pot.

White Chicken Chili

Andrea Pocreva
San Antonio, TX

Garnish with a sprinkle of crushed tortilla chips and a dollop of sour cream.

6 15-1/2 oz. cans Great
   Northern beans, drained
   and rinsed
3 5-oz. cans chicken, drained
6 c. chicken broth
3 c. shredded Monterey Jack
   cheese
2 4-oz. cans diced green chiles

12-oz. container sour cream
1 T. olive oil
2 t. ground cumin
1 t. garlic powder
1-1/2 t. dried oregano
1/4 t. white pepper
Optional: 2 onions, chopped

Combine all ingredients in a large stockpot. Simmer for 20 minutes until heated through. Serves 16 to 20.

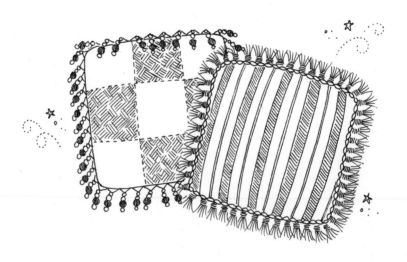

Check your local craft store for the newest fringe trims.
Ranging from homespun yarn fringe to fanciful beaded trims,
they're a quick & easy way to dress up your sofa pillows.

Easy Goulash

Kimberly Basore
Garland, TX

Replace the kidney beans with navy beans, if you prefer.

1 lb. ground beef
1/4 c. onion, chopped
14-1/2 oz. can stewed tomatoes
3/4 c. water
salt and pepper to taste
2 c. elbow macaroni, uncooked

15-1/4 oz. can corn, drained
15-oz. can kidney beans,
  drained and rinsed
16-oz. pkg. pasteurized
  processed cheese spread,
  cubed

Brown beef and onion in a large stockpot; drain. Add tomatoes and
water; sprinkle with salt and pepper to taste. Add macaroni and
simmer for 8 to 10 minutes or until macaroni is tender, adding more
water if necessary. Add corn, beans and cheese; heat until cheese is
melted. Serves 4 to 6.

Watch for old-fashioned clear glass canisters at tag sales
and flea markets...perfect countertop storage for
pasta and dried beans.

French Onion Soup

Barbara Feist Stienstra
Goshen, NY

The best French onion soup you'll ever eat! This recipe was created at the college where I worked for many years.

1 T. butter
2 T. olive oil
4 onions, sliced
3 c. beef broth

3 to 4 bay leaves
salt and pepper to taste
6 slices French bread, toasted
3/4 c. shredded Swiss cheese

Heat butter and oil in a stockpot over medium heat until butter melts. Add onions; cook for 20 to 30 minutes, until dark golden. Add broth, bay leaves, salt and pepper. Bring to a boil; reduce heat, cover and simmer for 30 minutes. Discard bay leaves. Ladle soup into 6 oven-safe soup bowls; top each with a slice of bread and sprinkle with cheese. Set bowls on a sturdy baking sheet. Broil until cheese is melted and golden. Serves 6.

Shake up family favorite noodle dishes by using different styles of pasta. Add interest with curly corkscrews, cavatelli shells or wagon wheels...even spinach-flavored or rainbow pasta.

Farmer's Dinner

Karen Jones
Lebanon, OH

A simple down-home dish to satisfy hearty appetites.

1 lb. bacon, cut in 2-inch pieces
2 14-1/2 oz. cans green beans,
    drained
15-1/4 oz. can corn, drained

6 potatoes, peeled and cubed
1-1/4 t. celery salt
1/2 t. salt
1/4 t. pepper

Heat bacon in a large stockpot until tender, but not crisp. Drain half of drippings; add remaining ingredients. Mix well; cover and simmer for 2-1/2 to 3 hours. Serves 4 to 6.

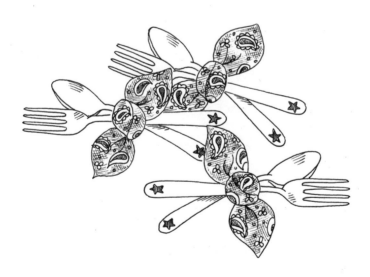

Carry out a country theme in your place settings.
Simply wrap a bright red bandanna around each set of
tableware and tie a big knot.

Lentil-Barley Vegetable Stew

Carrie Knotts
Kalispell, MT

When my grandmother "MaMaw Lou" passed away, all I wanted were her cookbooks. I found this recipe in one of them and just love it.

4 carrots, peeled and diced
2 leeks, diced
2 stalks celery, diced
2 zucchini, diced
1 onion, chopped
1/2 c. okra, sliced
1 c. lentils, uncooked

1/2 c. pearl barley, uncooked
6 to 7 c. vegetable broth
1 c. fresh basil, torn
1/4 c. olive oil
1 T. garlic, minced
1 t. dried thyme

Combine all ingredients in a large pot. Bring to a boil; reduce heat to medium and simmer until lentils and barley are tender, about 30 minutes. Serves 4.

Turn an old wagon wheel into a mini herb garden right outside your kitchen door. Plant marjoram, thyme, chives, sage and other fragrant herbs between the spokes, ready for snipping.

3-Bean Ravioli Minestrone

Staci Meyers
Cocoa, FL

A meatless main dish that's good and good for you...replace the chicken broth with vegetable broth if you wish.

1 onion, chopped
2 carrots, peeled and chopped
2 stalks celery, sliced
2 cloves garlic, minced
1 T. olive oil
3 14-1/2 oz. cans chicken broth
10-oz. pkg. frozen baby lima
  beans
15-oz. can kidney beans,
  drained and rinsed

15-1/2 oz. can garbanzo beans,
  drained and rinsed
2 14-1/2 oz. cans diced
  tomatoes
2 t. Italian seasoning
1/2 t. salt
1 t. pepper
7-oz. pkg. mini cheese ravioli,
  cooked

Combine onion, carrots, celery, garlic and olive oil in a large stockpot. Sauté over medium-high heat for 10 minutes until tender, stirring often. Add broth, beans, tomatoes and seasonings. Reduce heat to medium; simmer for 20 minutes. Stir in cooked ravioli just before serving. Makes 4 to 6 servings.

For a bountiful centerpiece, fill a basket with colorful peppers, carrots, redskin potatoes and squash.

Cheesy Rotini & Broccoli

Marian Buckley
Fontana, CA

Replace the broccoli with asparagus tips for variety.

1-1/2 c. rotini pasta, uncooked
2 carrots, peeled and sliced
1 c. broccoli flowerets
10-3/4 oz. can Cheddar cheese
    soup

1/2 c. milk
1/2 c. shredded Cheddar cheese
1 T. mustard

Cook pasta according to package directions. Add carrots and broccoli during last 5 minutes of cooking time; drain and return to pot. Pour soup, milk, cheese and mustard into pasta mixture; heat through. Serves 4.

Rigatoni with Blue Cheese

Zoe Bennett
Columbia, SC

Feel free to substitute your favorite tube pasta like penne or mostaccioli.

16-oz. pkg. rigatoni pasta,
    uncooked
2 T. butter

1/2 c. crumbled blue cheese
2 T. grated Parmesan cheese
pepper to taste

Cook rigatoni according to package directions; drain and return to pot. Add butter and cheeses; stir to mix until melted. Sprinkle with pepper to taste. Serves 4 to 6.

Chicken Pot au Feu

Pat Stotter
Scarsdale, NY

Pot on the Fire…a hearty French country dish. Serve the hot broth as a warming first course, with plenty of crusty bread for dipping.

2 t. olive oil
3 to 4 lbs. chicken
6 c. chicken broth
2 cloves garlic, thinly sliced
1 t. coriander seed, crushed
4 carrots, peeled and cut in
   2-inch pieces

8 new potatoes, halved
4 leeks, cut in 2-inch pieces
1 onion, quartered
1/2 t. salt
pepper to taste
Garnish: fresh Italian parsley,
   chopped

Heat oil in a stockpot over medium-high heat. Add chicken pieces and heat until golden, about 4 minutes per side. Remove chicken from pot; set aside. Put broth, garlic and coriander into pot; bring to a boil. Return chicken to pot; reduce heat, partially cover and simmer for 20 minutes. Add vegetables, salt and pepper to taste; partially cover and simmer for 20 minutes. Remove chicken and vegetables from pot with a slotted spoon; arrange on serving platter. Sprinkle with parsley. Serve broth separately, if desired. Serves 6.

I never met a meal I didn't like!
-Miss Piggy

Chorizo & Potato Stew

*Angela Murphey
Tempe, AZ*

If your supermarket doesn't have Mexican chorizo sausage, mild or spicy Italian sausage will work equally well.

2 onions, diced
2 red peppers, diced
1 T. garlic, minced
2 bay leaves
2 T. olive oil
salt to taste
3-1/2 lbs. new potatoes, cubed

1 lb. chorizo sausage, sliced
4 c. chicken broth
1/2 c. water
1-1/2 t. paprika
1/2 t. red pepper flakes
1 t. pepper
2 T. fresh parsley, minced

Sauté onions, peppers, garlic and bay leaves in olive oil for 2 to 3 minutes in a large soup pot. Add salt to taste; continue cooking, covered, over low heat for 15 minutes. Add potatoes and sausage; sauté for 2 minutes over medium heat. Add broth, water, paprika, red pepper flakes and pepper. Bring to a boil; reduce heat to medium and continue cooking, uncovered, for 20 minutes. Add parsley; continue cooking for 10 to 15 minutes or until potatoes are tender. Cover and let stand for 5 minutes. Discard bay leaves before serving. Serves 8.

Jambo

Megan Brooks
Antioch, TN

Not quite gumbo and not quite jambalaya, this dish is great with cornbread.

3 c. Kielbasa, thinly sliced
28-oz. can diced tomatoes
3 c. water
2 zucchini, halved and sliced
1/2 c. okra, sliced

1/2 c. green beans, cut in
    2-inch pieces
2 bay leaves
hot pepper sauce to taste
3 to 4 c. prepared rice

Combine all ingredients except hot pepper sauce and rice in a soup pot; bring to a boil. Reduce heat and simmer for 20 to 25 minutes; remove and discard bay leaves. Add hot pepper sauce to taste; serve over prepared rice. Makes 4 servings.

Cook a double batch of rice, then freeze half in a plastic freezer bag for another meal. When you're ready to use the frozen rice, just microwave on high for one minute per cup to thaw, 2 to 3 minutes per cup to warm it through. Fluff with a fork...ready to use!

Hearty Turkey-Veggie Soup

Lynn Williams
Muncie, IN

Chock-full of vegetables and turkey...a soup to be thankful for!

1 T. olive oil
2 t. garlic, minced
35-oz. can diced tomatoes
1-1/2 lbs. potatoes, peeled and diced
2 carrots, peeled and diced
12-oz. jar pearl onions, drained
2 stalks celery, sliced
8-oz. pkg. sliced mushrooms

1 t. dried thyme
1/2 t. dried rosemary
2 bay leaves
1/2 t. salt
2-1/2 lbs. skinless turkey thighs
10-oz. pkg. frozen peas, thawed
1-1/2 c. frozen corn, thawed
1/2 c. fresh parsley, minced
pepper to taste

Heat oil in a pressure cooker; add garlic and sauté 10 seconds. Add vegetables, herbs and salt. Place turkey, meaty-side down, over vegetables. Lock cooker lid and bring to 15 pounds of pressure over high heat. Adjust heat to maintain pressure and heat for 12 minutes with pressure regulator rocking slowly. Allow pressure to drop naturally; remove lid, tilting it away from you to allow excess steam to escape. Remove turkey from cooker. Discard bones and cut meat into bite-size pieces; return meat to cooker. Stir in peas, corn and parsley; simmer until heated through, about 3 to 5 minutes. Add pepper to taste. Discard bay leaves before serving. Serves 6.

Bread bowls make a hearty soup special. Cut the tops off round loaves of bread and hollow out, then rub with olive oil and garlic. Slip into the oven for 10 minutes at 400 degrees until crusty and golden. Ladle in soup and enjoy!

Chicken Viennese

Wendy Jacobs
Idaho Falls, ID

Garnish with a sprinkling of poppy seed.

2 T. butter
3 lbs. chicken
2 carrots, peeled and sliced
2 tomatoes, chopped
1 onion, chopped
1 green pepper, chopped

4-oz. can mushrooms, drained
1/2 c. chicken broth
salt and pepper to taste
1 T. all-purpose flour
3/4 c. sour cream
2 to 3 c. prepared rice or noodles

Melt butter in a pressure cooker. Add chicken pieces; heat until golden on both sides. Add vegetables, broth, salt and pepper. Secure lid; bring to 15 pounds of pressure. Cook for 10 minutes with pressure regulator rocking slowly. Allow pressure to drop naturally or cool at once by running cool water over top of cooker until pressure is reduced. Remove chicken and vegetables to a serving platter; set aside. Stir flour and sour cream into drippings. Cook and stir until mixture thickens; pour over chicken. Serve with prepared rice or noodles. Serves 4 to 6.

family
dinner
@ 6:00!

Turn favorite photos into a family fridge display.
Buy self-adhesive magnetic sheets at a photo shop, peel off
the backs and stick on photos of your children, friends and
pets. Your kids can cut out the figures in the photos for
instant shaped photo magnets.

Shrimp Jambalaya

Vickie

A spicy, savory blend of flavors that's good enough for company.

2 to 3 T. oil
1 clove garlic, chopped
1/2 c. onion, chopped
14-1/2 oz. can diced tomatoes
6-oz. can sliced mushrooms
1/2 lb. cooked ham, diced
1 c. long-cooking rice, uncooked
1/2 c. water
2 t. salt
1/8 t. pepper
1/8 t. allspice
1/8 t. cayenne pepper
1/8 t. chili powder
1/8 t. dried basil
16-oz. pkg. frozen salad shrimp, thawed
1/2 green pepper, cut into strips

Place oil, garlic and onion in a pressure cooker; sauté until golden. Add tomatoes, mushrooms, ham, rice, water, salt and spices; mix well. Add shrimp and green pepper; close lid securely and bring to 15 pounds of pressure. Place pressure regulator on vent pipe; cook 5 minutes with pressure regulator rocking slowly. Cool cooker at once by running cool water over top until pressure is reduced. Remove cover and stir; let stand 5 minutes before serving. Makes 4 to 6 servings.

A brand-new plastic sand pail makes a whimsical serving container for bread sticks.

Lemony Cod & New Potatoes

Mary Murray
Mt. Vernon, OH

The catch of the day, ready to eat in just a few minutes!

3 lbs. frozen cod fillets, thawed
1-1/2 t. lemon pepper
dill weed to taste
salt to taste

1-1/2 c. water
12 new potatoes, quartered
6 c. broccoli flowerets

Cut cod into 12 pieces; sprinkle with lemon pepper, dill weed and salt. Pour water into pressure cooker; arrange fish, potatoes and broccoli on cooking rack. Cover tightly; place pressure regulator on vent pipe and bring to 15 pounds of pressure. Cook 2 minutes with pressure regulator rocking slowly. Cool cooker at once by running cool water over top until pressure is reduced. Serves 6.

fresh DILL

Dad's Halupki Stuffed Cabbage

M.J. Owens
Albuquerque, NM

Our dad was of Russian descent. His mom made this recipe for him when he was growing up. He taught our mom how to make it and they in turn passed it down to all 9 of their children.

1 lb. ground beef
1 egg, beaten
4 to 5 slices bread, torn and
   moistened with water
14-oz. pkg. instant rice,
   uncooked

salt and pepper to taste
1 lb. bacon, crisply cooked and
   crumbled
1 onion, chopped
1 head cabbage, cored and
   boiled

Mix together ground beef, egg, bread, rice, salt and pepper in a large mixing bowl. Add bacon and onion; blend well. Stuff each cabbage leaf with mixture and roll up, being sure to tuck the ends into the roll. Place in a pressure cooker; cover tightly and place pressure regulator on vent pipe. Bring to 15 pounds of pressure and cook for 20 minutes. Cool cooker at once by running cool water over top until pressure is reduced. Serves 4 to 6.

Take time to share family stories and traditions with your kids! A cherished family recipe can be a great conversation starter at dinner.

New England Boiled Dinner

Anna McMaster
Portland, OR

Great-Grandmother's favorite one-pot meal...brought up-to-date with teriyaki sauce.

3-lb. beef brisket
1/2 c. teriyaki sauce
2 c. water, divided
4 new redskin potatoes
4 carrots, peeled and quartered

2 c. turnips, peeled and sliced
2 onions, quartered
1 lb. cabbage, cut into 6 to
   8 wedges

Place brisket in a large plastic zipping bag; sprinkle with teriyaki sauce. Refrigerate for one to 2 days, turning 2 to 3 times. Pour one cup water into pressure cooker; remove brisket from bag and place on cooking rack. Discard bag and sauce. Secure pressure cooker lid tightly; place regulator on vent pipe. Cook for 40 minutes at 15 pounds pressure with regulator rocking slowly. Let pressure drop naturally. Remove brisket and keep warm; add remaining water to cooker. Arrange vegetables on rack; close cover and regain 15 pounds pressure. Cook for 3 minutes with regulator rocking slowly; cool cooker at once by running cool water over top until pressure is reduced. Slice brisket thinly; arrange on platter surrounded by vegetables. Serves 8.

Pick up holiday paper plates at post-holiday sales and tuck them away. Use these plates to serve dinners on extra-busy pre-holiday nights...Easter, the 4th of July, Halloween, Thanksgiving and Christmas. No dishes to wash!

Skillet Dinner Math

Stir up a quick & hearty meal with foods you have on hand!

Meat		Veggies		Starch		Sauce		Add-Ins		Your Dinner
1 lb. cooked	+	1-1/2 to 2 c. fresh, canned or frozen	+	1 c. uncooked	+	1 can + 1-1/2 c. water or milk	+	to taste	=	
ground beef	+	corn	+	rice	+	tomato soup	+	salsa	=	Mexi-Beef & Rice
chicken, chopped	+	mixed veggies	+	elbow macaroni, rotini or penne pasta	+	cream of chicken soup	+	refrigerated biscuits (add 10 minutes before done; re-cover)	=	Skillet Chicken Pot Pie
ham, cubed	+	green beans	+	canned navy beans	+	cream of mushroom soup	+	garlic powder	=	Ham & 2-Bean Dinner
canned tuna, drained	+	mushrooms, sliced	+	egg noodles	+	cream of broccoli soup	+	dried, minced onion	=	Stovetop Tuna & Noodles
Kielbasa, sliced	+	broccoli, chopped	+	potatoes, diced	+	cream of celery soup	+	shredded cheese (add at end of cooking time)	=	Cheesy Sausage & Potatoes

Choose one from each group...go straight across or mix 'em up. Stir together in a skillet over medium heat. Bring to a boil; lower heat, cover and simmer 30 minutes, stirring occasionally. Serves 4.

Use this handy formula to stir up quick meals with what you have on hand. Just copy, cut and hang on the fridge or inside a cabinet door for easy reference!

Dinner's in the Oven

CASSEROLES, FOIL PACKAGES & ROASTING BAGS

Special Spanish Pot Roast

Linda Newkirk
Central Point, OR

A good friend shared this recipe with me years ago. I've prepared it many times for family and guests.

3-lb. beef pot roast
8-oz. bottle Catalina salad
  dressing, divided
6 to 8 carrots, peeled and diced

6 to 8 potatoes, peeled and diced
Optional: 1 onion, quartered
12-oz. jar olives with pimentos

Heat 1/4 cup dressing in an oven-safe pan over medium heat. Add roast to pan; heat and turn until all sides are browned. Add carrots, potatoes and onion, if using, to pan. Pour remaining dressing over all; top with olives and olive juice. Cover and bake at 350 degrees for 2 to 3 hours to desired doneness. Serves 4 to 6.

Baked Pot Roast & Gravy

Mandy Lasley
Jellico, TN

My husband's favorite...the longer it bakes, the better!

3 to 4-lb. beef pot roast
salt and meat tenderizer to taste
2 10-3/4 oz. cans golden
  mushroom soup, divided
1-1/2 oz. pkg. onion soup mix

3-1/4 c. water, divided
5 to 6 potatoes, peeled and
  cubed
16-oz. pkg. baby carrots
1 to 2 onions, sliced

Place roast in a roasting pan; sprinkle with salt and meat tenderizer to taste. Stir together one can mushroom soup, onion soup mix and water; pour over roast. Add additional water, if necessary, to cover roast. Bake at 350 degrees for 1-1/2 to 2 hours. Add remaining can of soup and vegetables to pan. Bake an additional 30 minutes, until vegetables are tender. Serves 6 to 8.

Country-Style Turkey Pot Roast

Tina Stidam
Delaware, OH

This pot roast makes its own delicious thick gravy. The recipe works well with other meats too.

2 to 3 T. oil
6 to 8-lb. skinless turkey breast
salt to taste
6 potatoes, peeled and quartered
6 to 8 carrots, peeled and halved
3 turnips, peeled and quartered
2 stalks celery, quartered
2 onions, halved
1/2 head cabbage, quartered
2 3-oz. pkgs. brown gravy mix
1-1/2 oz. pkg. onion soup mix
2-1/4 c. water

Heat oil in a roaster pan over medium heat; add turkey breast and sauté on all sides until golden. Sprinkle with salt to taste. Add vegetables to roaster; set aside. Combine gravy and soup mixes with water; pour over turkey and vegetables. Cover and bake at 350 degrees for 2 to 3 hours, depending on size of breast, basting with pan juices after 1-1/2 hours. Serves 8 to 10.

Create a family art gallery. Spray-paint a bulletin board a bright color and decorate the frame with textured paint. Glue buttons or charms to thumbtacks with craft glue, then display your children's drawings and paintings with pride.

Chicken à la Kym

Joann Britton
Chesterfield, MO

This recipe was my daughter's favorite recipe for company.
I'm sending it in honor of her teenage daughter.

4 boneless, skinless chicken
    breasts, halved
8 slices Swiss cheese
10-3/4 oz. can cream of chicken
    soup

1/4 c. white wine or chicken
    broth
1 c. chicken-flavored stuffing
    mix
1/4 c. butter, melted

Arrange chicken in a lightly greased 13"x9" baking dish; top with
cheese slices. Combine soup, wine or broth and stuffing mix; spread
over chicken. Drizzle with butter; bake at 350 degrees for 55 minutes.
Makes 6 to 8 servings.

Let your kids plan the family dinner once a week. Younger
children can practice basic cooking skills, while older kids
and teens might enjoy choosing and preparing
ethnic or specialty meals.

Pixie's Chicken Casserole

Kelly Elliott
Burns, TN

Pixie is a dear family friend who served this easy-yet-elegant dish at a bridal luncheon in my honor.

4 c. cooked chicken, cubed
2 c. celery, diced
2 10-3/4 oz. cans cream of
 chicken soup
1-1/2 c. mayonnaise

2 c. prepared rice
1 T. dried, minced onion
salt and pepper to taste
1 c. cashew halves
2 c. chow mein noodles

Combine all ingredients except cashews and noodles in a lightly greased 13"x9" casserole dish. Top with cashews and noodles; bake at 375 degrees for 40 minutes. Serves 6 to 8.

Give frozen ready-to-bake dinner rolls a homemade touch.
Before baking, brush rolls with egg beaten with a little water.
Sprinkle with sesame seed or coarse salt and bake as usual.

Baked Chicken Reuben

Doris Reichard
Baltimore, MD

How clever...our favorite deli sandwich flavors in a casserole!

4 boneless, skinless chicken
  breasts
1/4 t. salt
1/8 t. pepper
2 c. sauerkraut, drained

8-oz. bottle Russian salad
  dressing
4 slices Swiss cheese
1 T. dried parsley
Garnish: fresh chives, chopped

Arrange chicken breasts in a greased 13"x9" baking dish; sprinkle
with salt and pepper. Spread sauerkraut over chicken; pour dressing
evenly over all. Top with cheese slices and parsley; cover and bake
at 350 degrees for one hour or until tender. Sprinkle with chives.
Serves 4.

When you carry a lidded casserole to a potluck, use
2 large rubber bands to hold the lid on securely. Stretch a
rubber band over the knob on the lid and pull over the
handles on one side; repeat on the other side with a
second rubber band.

Saucy Chicken & Rice

Jeanne Berfiend
Indianapolis, IN

Add a teaspoon of dried thyme for a savory touch.

10-3/4 oz. can cream of
    mushroom soup
10-3/4 oz. can cream of chicken
    soup
10-3/4 oz. can cream of celery
    soup

1-3/4 c. instant rice, uncooked
1-1/2 oz. pkg. onion soup mix
2 c. water
6 boneless, skinless chicken
    breasts

Combine all ingredients except chicken in a 13"x9" baking pan. Gently push chicken breasts into the mixture until they are partly covered. Cover pan; bake at 350 degrees for 1-1/2 hours. Uncover and bake an additional 30 minutes. Serves 6.

Give little artists their own chalkboard wall. Mark off a big square with masking tape and brush on chalkboard paint, following product instructions. A length of wooden molding underneath holds colored chalk and an eraser.

Ham & Swiss Cheese Rolls

Janet Stewart
Owensboro, KY

This recipe is a favorite at our Mothers of Preschoolers (MOPS) church group.

3/4 c. margarine
1-1/2 T. Worcestershire sauce
1/2 t. dry mustard
1-1/2 t. poppy seed

2 t. dried, minced onion
2 12-ct. pkgs. Hawaiian rolls
1 lb. thinly sliced deli ham
1/2 lb. sliced Swiss cheese

Combine margarine, Worcestershire sauce, mustard, poppy seed and onion in a small saucepan. Bring to a boil over medium heat; remove from heat. Slice individual rolls in half. Make sandwiches using bread, ham and cheese. Place sandwiches on an ungreased 15"x10" jelly-roll pan. Spoon margarine mixture over sandwiches. Bake, uncovered, at 350 degrees for 15 minutes. Makes 12 servings.

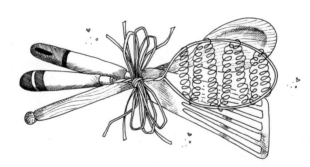

Everyday items can become not-so-ordinary wall displays. Look for kitchen utensils or garden tools at tag sales and flea markets. For added interest, frame a favorite photo of your family gardening or cooking together.

Golden Parmesan Roasted Potatoes Linda Hendrix
Moundville, MO

Pop into the oven alongside a roast for
a homestyle dinner that can't be beat.

1/4 c. all-purpose flour	6 potatoes, peeled and cut into
1/4 c. grated Parmesan cheese	wedges
3/4 t. salt	1/3 c. butter, melted
1/8 t. pepper	Garnish: fresh parsley, chopped

Place flour, cheese, salt and pepper in a large plastic zipping bag; mix well. Add potato wedges; shake to coat. Pour butter into a 13"x9" baking pan, tilting to coat; arrange potatoes in pan. Bake, uncovered, at 375 degrees for one hour. Sprinkle with parsley. Serves 4 to 6.

Keep browned ground beef on hand for easy meal prep. Crumble several pounds of beef onto a baking pan and bake at 350 degrees until browned through, stirring often. Drain well and pack recipe portions in freezer bags.

Fiesta Bubble Bread

Amy Hunt
Traphill, NC

A little spicy and loaded with cheesy goodness...a delicious side!

1/2 c. butter, melted
1-1/2 c. shredded Mexican-
blend cheese
1/4 c. shredded mozzarella
cheese

10-oz. jar sliced jalapeño
peppers, drained
1 t. dried parsley
2 12-oz. tubes refrigerated
biscuits, cut into quarters

In a large bowl, combine butter, cheeses, pepper slices and parsley; add biscuits and toss to coat. Transfer to an ungreased Bundt® pan. Bake at 350 degrees for 30 minutes, or until golden. Invert onto a serving plate; serve warm. Serves 8.

Homestyle Tuna Pot Pie

Elaine Nichols
Mesa, AZ

For a whimsical touch, use a fish-shaped cookie cutter to cut the vents in the top crust.

2 9-inch pie crusts, divided
12-1/2 oz. can tuna, drained
10-3/4 oz. can cream of potato
soup
10-oz. pkg. frozen peas &
carrots

1/2 c. onion, chopped
1/3 c. milk
1/2 t. dried thyme
salt and pepper to taste

Line an 8"x8" baking pan with one pie crust. Combine remaining ingredients and pour into crust; top with remaining crust. Seal and crimp the edges; slit the top of the crust to vent. Bake at 375 degrees for 50 minutes or until golden. Serves 4 to 6.

Country Chicken Pot Pie

Kris Coburn
Dansville, NY

Just like Mom used to make! It's a delicious way to use up leftover chicken and cooked vegetables too.

2 9-inch pie crusts, divided
1-1/2 c. cooked chicken, diced
2 to 3 c. frozen mixed
   vegetables, thawed
2 10-3/4 oz. cans cream of
   chicken soup

1/2 c. milk
1 t. pepper
1 t. dried thyme
1 egg, beaten

Line a 9" pie plate with one crust. Mix together chicken, vegetables, soup, milk, pepper and thyme; spread in crust. Top with remaining crust; cut slits to vent and brush with egg. Bake at 350 degrees for 50 minutes, or until golden. Serves 4 to 6.

There is nothing better on a cold wintry day than
a properly made pot pie.
-Craig Claiborne

Spicy Sausage & Chicken Creole

Carrie Knotts
Kalispell, MT

I used this dish to win over my husband and his family while we were dating. He likes his food spicy! Of course, you can use a little less hot pepper sauce if you prefer.

14-1/2 oz. can chopped
   tomatoes
1/2 c. long-cooking rice,
   uncooked
1/2 c. hot water
2 t. hot pepper sauce
1/4 t. garlic powder
1/4 t. dried oregano

16-oz. pkg. frozen broccoli, corn
   & red pepper blend, thawed
4 boneless, skinless chicken
   thighs
1/2 lb. link Italian sausage,
   cooked and quartered
8-oz. can tomato sauce

Combine tomatoes, rice, water, hot sauce and seasonings in a
13"x9" baking dish. Cover and bake at 375 degrees for 10 minutes.
Stir vegetables into tomato mixture; top with chicken and sausage.
Pour tomato sauce over top. Bake, covered, at 375 degrees for
40 minutes or until juices of chicken run clear. Serves 4.

Try drying fresh herbs from your garden…so easy! Simply
cut bunches and tie with jute, then hang on a peg rack. The
herbs will dry naturally and lend a country look to your
kitchen. Pinch off sprigs to add flavor to recipes.

Chicken-Zucchini Bake

Julie Brown
Provo, UT

This recipe proves there's no such thing as too many zucchini!

1 T. margarine, melted
12-oz. pkg. chicken-flavored
   stuffing mix
6 c. zucchini, sliced and steamed
1 c. carrots, peeled and grated

3 to 4 lbs. cooked chicken, diced
10-3/4 oz. can cream of chicken
   soup
1 c. sour cream
1/4 c. onion, chopped

Combine margarine and stuffing mix; spoon half of mixture in the bottom of a 13"x9" baking pan. Layer zucchini, carrots and chicken over the top; set aside. Mix soup, sour cream and onion together; spoon over chicken. Top with remaining stuffing mix; bake at 350 degrees for 45 minutes. Serves 6 to 8.

A simple crockery bowl filled to the brim with ripe pears, apples and other fresh fruit makes an oh-so-simple centerpiece...a great way to encourage healthy snacking too!

Cheesy Sausage-Potato Casserole

J.J. Presley
Portland, TX

Add some fresh green beans too, if you like.

3 to 4 potatoes, sliced
2 8-oz. links sausage, sliced
    into 2-inch lengths

1 onion, chopped
1/2 c. butter, sliced
1 c. shredded Cheddar cheese

Layer potatoes, sausage and onion in a 13"x9" baking pan sprayed with non-stick vegetable spray. Dot with butter; sprinkle with cheese. Bake at 350 degrees for 1-1/2 hours. Serves 6 to 8.

Jars of jewel-colored preserves deserve to be shown off!
Display golden apricot jam, ruby red pickled beets and
bright green dill pickles on a sunny windowsill.

Deep-Dish Skillet Pizza

Linda Kilgore
Kittanning, PA

This recipe is my husband's. He made us one of these pizzas for supper and now it's the only pizza we ever want to eat. Delicious!

1 loaf frozen bread dough, thawed
1 to 2 15-oz. jars pizza sauce
1/2 lb. ground pork sausage, browned and drained
5-oz. pkg. sliced pepperoni

1/2 c. sliced mushrooms
1/2 c. green pepper, sliced
Italian seasoning to taste
1 c. shredded mozzarella cheese
1 c. shredded Cheddar cheese

Generously grease a large cast-iron skillet. Press thawed dough into the bottom and up the sides of skillet. Spread desired amount of pizza sauce over dough. Add favorite toppings, ending with cheeses on top. Bake at 425 degrees for 30 minutes. Carefully remove skillet from oven. Let stand several minutes; pizza will finish baking in the skillet. Cut into wedges to serve. Serves 4.

A tasty apple coleslaw goes well with pork. Simply toss together a large bag of coleslaw mix, a chopped Granny Smith apple and one cup of mayonnaise.

Kielbasa Bean Pot

Sharon Crider
Lebanon, MO

So easy to prepare...so flavorful and filling.

2 16-oz. cans pork & beans
1-1/2 oz. pkg. onion soup mix
1/3 c. catsup
1/4 c. water

2 t. brown sugar
1 T. mustard
1 lb. Kielbasa, sliced

Combine all ingredients in a 2-quart baking dish. Bake, uncovered, at 350 degrees for one hour. Serves 6 to 8.

Warm up a loaf of fresh bread from the bakery...so tasty served with plenty of butter! Simply wrap in aluminum foil and bake at 350 degrees for a few minutes until warmed through.

Mac & Cheese Cupcakes

Shelley Turner
Boise, ID

*I like to make these on the weekends and then pop them
in the microwave when I see the kids get off the bus.*

8-oz. pkg. elbow macaroni,
  cooked
1 t. olive oil
1-1/2 c. milk
2 T. cornstarch
1 t. Dijon mustard

salt and pepper to taste
2 c. shredded sharp Cheddar
  cheese
1/2 c. seasoned dry bread
  crumbs

Toss macaroni with olive oil; set aside. In a medium saucepan, whisk
milk and cornstarch until blended. Bring to a boil over medium heat,
stirring often. Stir in mustard, salt and pepper. Reduce heat and
simmer until thickened, stirring frequently. Add cheese and stir until
melted; fold in macaroni. Grease 12 muffin cups with butter, coat with
bread crumbs and shake off excess. Spoon in macaroni mixture. Bake
at 350 degrees for 15 to 25 minutes, until golden. Makes one dozen.

Make a potato print tablecloth...fun for the kids! Cut a
potato in half and let them draw simple designs like flowers
or stars on the cut surfaces. Cut around the designs with a
blunt knife, then pour fabric paint in a paper plate and let 'em
stamp away on a plain tablecloth.

Easy Beef Burgundy

Laurie Aitken
Walden, NY

A simple-to-make version of this classic dish...great for company.

2 lbs. stew beef, cubed
2 10-3/4 oz. cans cream of
   mushroom soup
2 4-oz. cans mushrooms,
   drained

2 c. red wine or beef broth
1-1/2 oz. pkg. onion soup mix
3 to 4 c. prepared egg noodles

Combine all ingredients except noodles in a 2-quart baking dish. Bake at 350 degrees for 3 hours, stirring occasionally. Serve over prepared noodles. Serves 6 to 8.

It's so easy to double casserole recipes and freeze half for another night. When you're busy or just don't feel like cooking, you'll have a warm, yummy meal.

Oven Chicken Cordon Bleu

Heather Webb
Richmond, VA

Pecans lend a crunchy touch to this favorite.

4 boneless, skinless chicken
   breasts
4 t. Dijon mustard, divided
1 t. garlic, minced and divided

4 slices deli ham
4 slices Swiss cheese
olive oil
1 c. chopped pecans

Pound chicken breasts flat; top each with one teaspoon mustard and
1/4 teaspoon garlic. Place one slice ham and one slice cheese on each
breast; roll up each breast and secure with toothpicks. Brush each roll
with oil; roll in pecans. Place in a 13"x9" baking pan; bake at
350 degrees for 35 to 40 minutes. Serves 4.

Shake up some fresh herbed vinaigrette dressing.
In a jar, combine 3/4 cup olive oil, 1/4 cup white wine
vinegar, 1/4 cup fresh basil, 1/4 cup fresh parsley and
a tablespoon of sliced green onions. Shake well and
toss with salad greens.

Grecian Chicken

Lisa Hains
Tipp City, OH

I like to put this in the oven before leaving for church.

8 boneless, skinless chicken
 breasts
8 to 10 potatoes, peeled and
 halved
8 to 10 carrots, peeled

2 T. dried rosemary
3 T. olive oil
3 T. lemon juice
salt and pepper to taste
1 t. garlic powder

Place chicken in a greased roasting pan; bake at 450 degrees until golden, about 20 minutes. Add potatoes and carrots to pan; pour in enough water to partially cover vegetables. Sprinkle with rosemary; drizzle with oil and lemon juice. Sprinkle with salt, pepper and garlic powder. Reduce oven to 350 degrees and bake, covered, about 3 hours until vegetables are tender. Serves 8.

For a quick Greek salad that will complement Grecian Chicken, toss together chopped tomato and cucumber with sliced black olives and crumbled feta cheese. Add oil & vinegar salad dressing.

Rooster Pie

Tammy Rowe
Bellevue, OH

The aroma of country goodness fills the house as it's baking...we can hardly wait to break the golden crust!

2 c. cooked chicken, cubed
1/2 c. frozen carrots
1/2 c. frozen peas
1 onion, diced
3 T. pimentos, chopped
1 T. fresh parsley, chopped
salt and pepper to taste

10-3/4 oz. can cream of chicken soup
1 c. sour cream
1 c. chicken broth
11-1/2 oz. tube refrigerated biscuits

Combine chicken, carrots, peas, onion, pimentos, parsley, salt and pepper; set aside. Combine soup, sour cream and broth; stir into chicken mixture. Spread in a greased 13"x9" casserole dish. Arrange biscuits over top. Bake at 350 degrees for 30 minutes, until biscuits are golden. Serves 4 to 6.

Pick up artist or event posters when your family visits museums or festivals to hang in your home...decorations that show off the memorable places you've been together.

·Dinner's in the Oven·

Spinach-Cheddar Quiche
Jo Ann

Try this recipe using a variety of other veggies like asparagus, mushrooms or artichokes. Great for brunch as well as dinner!

1 loaf Italian bread, torn into
    bite-size pieces
1 onion, chopped
2 10-oz. pkgs. frozen chopped
    spinach, thawed and drained
4 c. shredded Cheddar cheese

4 eggs, beaten
1-1/2 c. milk
salt, pepper and garlic powder
    to taste
Garnish: sour cream

Combine all ingredients except sour cream; pour into a greased 13"x9" baking pan. Bake at 350 degrees for 40 to 50 minutes until a knife inserted into the center comes out clean. Cut into squares; serve with sour cream on the side. Makes 6 to 8 servings.

For conversation-starter placemats, arrange family photos, kids' drawings, stickers and other items on colorful poster board, using a glue stick to attach. Add swirls of colorful jute or rick-rack for a charming touch. Press on self-adhesive clear plastic for wipe-clean ease.

Turkey-Spinach Quiche

Jenny Poole
Salisbury, NC

*This recipe is a holiday tradition at our house. I bake it in muffin
tins for a nice presentation...my guests love it.*

1 lb. ground turkey sausage,
   browned and drained
3 c. shredded Cheddar cheese
10-oz. pkg. frozen chopped
   spinach, cooked and drained
8-oz. can sliced mushrooms,
   drained

2/3 c. onion, chopped
1 c. mayonnaise
1 c. milk
4 eggs, beaten
1-1/4 c. biscuit baking mix
2 T. cornstarch

Mix all ingredients together and pour into a greased 9" pie plate.
Bake at 350 degrees for 35 to 40 minutes, until golden and set.
Serves 4 to 6.

kitchen
journal

Start a kitchen journal to note favorite recipes, family
preferences, even special dinner guests and celebrations. It'll
make planning meals much easier and later will become a
cherished keepsake.

Stuffed Cabbage Casserole

Kelly Schurdell
Strongsville, OH

If you like stuffed cabbage, you'll appreciate this quick & easy variation...no need to roll individual cabbage leaves.

10 c. cabbage, chopped and divided
2 lbs. ground beef
1/2 c. instant rice, uncooked
1 t. salt
1 t. garlic powder

3/4 c. sour cream
1 onion, chopped
2 10-3/4 oz. cans tomato soup
1/2 c. catsup
1 c. shredded Colby cheese

Place 5 cups cabbage in a greased 13"x9" casserole dish; set aside. Combine ground beef, rice, salt, garlic powder, sour cream and onion; spread over cabbage. Layer remaining cabbage over meat mixture; top with tomato soup, then catsup. Sprinkle with cheese; cover. Bake at 350 degrees for 2 hours. Serves 6 to 8.

Line the baking dish with aluminum foil whenever you plan to freeze a casserole...clean-up will be a snap!

Hobo Dinner

Denise Mainville
Elk Rapids, MI

My mom and I have made this recipe for years. It's quick, delicious and so easy the kids can help assemble it.

1-1/2 lbs. ground beef
1 t. Worcestershire sauce
1/2 t. seasoned pepper
1/8 t. garlic powder
3 redskin potatoes, sliced

1 onion, sliced
3 carrots, peeled and halved
olive oil and dried parsley
    to taste

Combine beef, Worcestershire sauce, pepper and garlic powder; form into 4 to 6 patties. Place each patty on an 18-inch length of aluminum foil. Divide slices of potato, onion and carrots evenly and place on each patty. Sprinkle with olive oil and parsley to taste. Wrap tightly in aluminum foil and arrange on a baking sheet; bake at 375 degrees for one hour. Serves 4 to 6.

Year 'round fun! Make a garden scarecrow by tying together long and short posts in a T-shape and adding a stuffed paper bag for a head. Give your scarecrow a seasonal wardrobe...an old shirt and straw hat for summer, a pumpkin head for fall, then a cast-off knit cap and muffler for winter.

Swiss Bliss

Brenda Doak
Delaware, OH

I've had this recipe over 30 years. It's great with mashed potatoes.

2 lbs. beef chuck roast, cut into
    4 to 6 pieces
1-1/2 oz. pkg. onion soup mix
16-oz. can chopped tomatoes,
    drained and 1/2 c. juice
    reserved
8-oz. pkg. sliced mushrooms

1/2 green pepper, sliced
1/4 t. salt
pepper to taste
1 T. steak sauce
1 T. cornstarch
1 T. fresh parsley, chopped

Arrange beef pieces, slightly overlapping, on a greased 20-inch length of aluminum foil. Sprinkle with onion soup mix; top with tomatoes, mushrooms, green pepper, salt and pepper. Mix together reserved tomato juice, steak sauce and cornstarch; pour over meat and vegetables. Fold aluminum foil up over all and double-fold edges to seal tightly. Place foil package in a baking pan. Bake at 375 degrees for 2 hours, until tender. Sprinkle with parsley. Serves 4 to 6.

Dress up instant mashed potatoes. Prepare a family-size portion, then stir in an 8-ounce package of cream cheese. Spoon into a baking dish and bake at 375 to 400 degrees for about 30 minutes, until golden.

Big Eddie's Rigatoni

Mary Beth Laporte
Escanaba, MI

This recipe was created by my eighty-four-year-old father who has always been a great cook and is affectionately called "Big Eddie" by family members. A delicious and satisfying meal when paired with salad and garlic bread.

16-oz. pkg. rigatoni pasta,
   uncooked
1/8 t. salt
2 lbs. lean ground beef
1-1/2 oz. pkg. spaghetti sauce
   mix
45-oz. jar chunky tomato, garlic
   and onion pasta sauce

8 slices mozzarella cheese,
   divided
8 slices provolone cheese,
   divided
8-oz. container sour cream
Garnish: grated Parmesan
   cheese

Cook pasta according to package directions; drain, mix in salt and set aside. Meanwhile, in a large, deep skillet over medium heat, brown ground beef; drain. Stir in spaghetti sauce mix and pasta sauce; heat through. In a greased 13"x9" baking pan, layer half the pasta, 4 slices mozzarella cheese and 4 slices provolone cheese. Spread entire container of sour cream across top. Layer half of ground beef mixture. Repeat layering, except for sour cream, ending with ground beef mixture. Garnish with Parmesan cheese. Bake, uncovered, at 350 degrees for 30 minutes, or until bubbly. Serves 8.

Start a Family Game Night! Get out all your favorite board games and play to your heart's content. Small prizes for winners and bowls of popcorn or snack mix are a must!

BINGO
Checkers
Family Games ☆

Spicy Pork Packets

Virginia Watson
Scranton, PA

Sometimes I replace the plain corn with a can of sweet corn & diced peppers to add a bit of extra color.

14-1/2 oz. can chicken broth
2 c. instant rice, uncooked
1-1/2 T. spicy taco mix, divided
1/8 t. cayenne pepper
1/8 t. salt

1/8 t. pepper
15-oz. can corn, drained
1/3 c. green onion, sliced
4 boneless pork chops

Heat broth to boiling in a medium saucepan; remove from heat. Add rice, one teaspoon taco mix, cayenne pepper, salt and pepper to taste. Cover and let stand for about 5 minutes until liquid is absorbed. Add corn and green onion; set aside. Sprinkle pork chops with remaining taco mix; place each on an 18-inch length of aluminum foil sprayed with non-stick cooking spray. Divide rice mixture evenly over pork chops; fold aluminum foil over to enclose food and seal tightly. Place packets on a baking sheet; cut an X to vent foil. Bake at 400 degrees for 45 minutes. Serves 4.

Use acrylic paint to write "Mom's Menu" or "Tonight's Specials" across the top of a small blackboard for your kitchen. Use chalk to update daily...let everyone know what's for dinner!

Mom's Menu

☆ Spicy Pork Packets
☆ Green Salad

for dessert:

☆ Apple crisp !

No-Muss Chicken Dinner

Tori Willis
Champaign, IL

This easy recipe makes its own delicious chicken gravy.

1 T. all-purpose flour
10-3/4 oz. can cream of
   mushroom soup
10-oz. pkg. frozen green beans,
   thawed
1/2 c. chicken broth

2.8-oz. can French fried onions,
   divided
6 boneless, skinless chicken
   breasts
seasoned salt and pepper
   to taste

Shake flour in a large oven bag; arrange in a 13"x9" baking pan.
Add soup, green beans, broth and half the onions to the bag. Sprinkle
chicken with seasoned salt and pepper to taste. Arrange chicken in
oven bag on top of soup mixture. Sprinkle remaining onions over
chicken. Close bag with nylon tie provided; cut six, 1/2-inch slits in
bag. Bake at 350 degrees for 45 to 50 minutes until chicken juices run
clear. Stir sauce in bag; spoon over chicken. Serves 6.

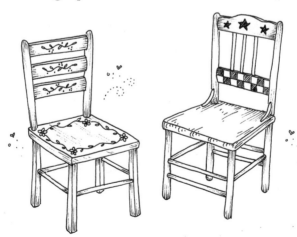

Unite mismatched tag sale chairs at your dining table by
painting them in a country color like barn red or robin's egg
blue. Distress them for the look of age, then stencil on stars,
flowers or even family members' names for a personal touch.

·Dinner's in the Oven·

Oh-So-Easy Chicken & Veggies

Laura Fuller
Fort Wayne, IN

Try this recipe with 3 turkey thighs, sweet potatoes and a bit of dried sage too.

2 T. all-purpose flour
2.6-oz. pkg. golden onion
   soup mix
1 c. water
3 carrots, peeled and diced
2 redskin potatoes, cut in
   wedges

1 green pepper, cubed
6 boneless, skinless chicken
   breasts
seasoned salt to taste
pepper to taste

Shake flour in a large oven bag; arrange bag in a 13"x9" baking pan. Add soup mix and water to bag; squeeze bag to blend flour. Add carrots, potatoes and green pepper; turn bag to coat ingredients. Sprinkle chicken with seasoned salt and pepper to taste; arrange in bag on top of vegetables. Close bag with nylon tie provided; cut six, 1/2-inch slits in top. Tuck ends of bag into pan. Bake at 350 degrees for 55 to 60 minutes until chicken is tender and juices run clear. Serves 4 to 6.

Build a simple bench from old barn siding for the instant look of a primitive flea-market find. It will be equally at home in the backyard for garden daydreaming or near the kitchen door where kids can sit on it to pull off their boots.

Country Beef Roast

Mylissa Gholson
Aspermont, TX

I like to fix this delicious meal and leave it roasting in the oven while I'm out in the barn.

2 T. all-purpose flour
3 to 5-lb. beef pot roast
1-1/2 oz. pkg. onion soup mix
10-3/4 oz. can cream of
   mushroom soup

1-1/4 c. water
6 to 8 potatoes, peeled
   and cubed
3 to 4 onions, sliced
4 to 6 carrots, peeled and sliced

Shake flour in a large oven bag; arrange bag in a roasting pan. Place roast into bag; top with soup mix, mushroom soup and water. Close with nylon tie provided; cut six, 1/2-inch slits in top. Bake at 325 degrees for 3 to 4 hours or until roast is fork tender. Add potatoes, onions and carrots to bag; reclose bag and bake an additional hour. Serve with pan drippings as gravy. Serves 10 to 12.

For dark, rich-looking gravy, add a spoonful or 2 of brewed coffee. It will add color to pale gravy but won't affect the flavor.

Western Pork Chops

Kerry Mayer
Dunham Springs, LA

For a delicious variation, try substituting peeled, cubed sweet potatoes for the redskins.

1 T. all-purpose flour	4 redskin potatoes, sliced
1 c. barbecue sauce	1 green pepper, cubed
4 pork chops	1 c. baby carrots
salt and pepper to taste	

Shake flour in a large oven bag; place in a 13"x9" baking pan. Add barbecue sauce to oven bag; squeeze bag to blend in flour. Season pork chops with salt and pepper; add pork chops and vegetables to oven bag. Turn bag to coat ingredients with sauce; arrange vegetables in an even layer with pork chops on top. Close bag with nylon tie provided; cut six, 1/2-inch slits in top. Bake at 350 degrees for about 40 to 45 minutes until pork chops and vegetables are tender. Serves 4.

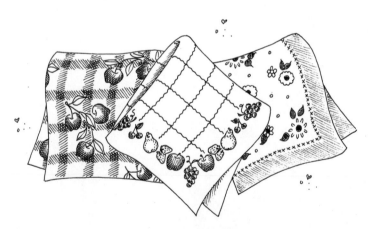

Bring out Mom's printed tablecloths from the 1950's and use them...they're too much fun to hide away! Red strawberries, cowboys & cowgirls, vacation spots and other whimsical designs will delight your kids and bring back fond memories of family meals years ago.

Beef Brisket in a Bag

Meg Venema
Kirkland, WA

Pineapple juice and soy sauce are the secret ingredients that make this brisket taste wonderful.

3 to 4-lb. beef brisket
pepper and paprika to taste
1 T. all-purpose flour

8-oz. can pineapple juice
3 T. soy sauce
1-1/2 oz. pkg. onion soup mix

Rub brisket with pepper and paprika. Shake flour in a large oven bag and place roast in bag, fat-side up. Place bag in a 13"x9" baking pan. Combine pineapple juice, soy sauce and soup mix; pour mixture over brisket. Close bag with nylon tie provided; cut six, 1/2-inch slits in top. Bake at 325 degrees for 3 hours. Remove from oven; place brisket on cutting board and pour remaining bag contents into the baking pan. Slice brisket against the grain; arrange slices over juices in baking pan. Baste with juices; cover pan with aluminum foil and return to oven for one additional hour, basting occasionally. Makes 6 to 8 servings.

Fill a low cupboard with unbreakable pans, bowls, measuring cups and utensils…little ones can enjoy "cooking" right alongside you.

Easy Sunday Chicken Dinner

Connie Hilty
Pearland, TX

This dinner is so simple to put in the oven before we leave for church...it's ready when we get back, and the house smells heavenly!

1 T. all-purpose flour
1 t. garlic salt, divided
1 lb. redskin potatoes
8-oz. pkg. baby carrots
2 stalks celery, sliced

1 onion, cut in wedges
4 to 5 lbs. chicken
1 T. oil
1 t. paprika

Shake flour and 1/2 teaspoon garlic salt in a large oven bag; place bag in a 13"x9" baking pan. Arrange vegetables in bag; turn to coat with flour. Push vegetables to outer edge of bag. Brush chicken with oil; sprinkle remaining garlic and paprika over chicken. Arrange chicken in bag in center of vegetables. Close bag with nylon tie provided; cut six, 1/2-inch slits in top of bag. Bake at 350 degrees for 1-1/2 hours, until chicken juices run clear. Serves 5 to 6.

They say a person needs just 3 things to be truly happy in this world: someone to love, something to do and something to hope for.
-Tom Bodett

South-of-the-Border Chicken

Penny Sherman
Cumming, GA

Scrumptious...makes any meal a fiesta!

2 T. all-purpose flour
14-1/2 oz. can diced tomatoes
   with chili seasoning
2 t. diced jalapeños
1/2 t. salt

15-oz. can black beans, drained
   and rinsed
6 boneless, skinless chicken
   breasts
1 yellow pepper, sliced

Shake flour in a large oven bag; place bag in a 13"x9" baking pan.
Add tomatoes, jalapeños and salt to bag; squeeze to blend with flour.
Add beans and chicken to bag; turn to coat chicken. Top with yellow
pepper. Close bag with nylon tie provided; cut six, 1/2-inch slits in top.
Bake at 350 degrees for 45 to 50 minutes, until chicken juices run
clear. Serves 4.

Serve homemade crispy tortilla chips with South-of-the-
Border Chicken! Simply cut corn tortillas into wedges, spritz
with non-stick vegetable spray and arrange on a baking sheet.
Sprinkle with salt and bake at 350 degrees until crisp, 5 to
10 minutes. Try seasoned salt or garlic salt for an extra kick.

Casserole Dinner Math

Nothing to eat? Not so fast! Check your cupboards & pop a tasty casserole in the oven.

Meat		Veggies		Starch		Sauce		Add-Ins		Your Dinner
1 lb. cooked	+	1-1/2 to 2 c. fresh or canned	+	2 c. cooked	+	1 to 2 cans	+	to taste	=	Oven Chili
ground beef	+	onion, chopped	+	canned kidney beans	+	tomato soup	+	salsa	=	Oven Chili
chicken, chopped	+	mushrooms, sliced	+	egg noodles	+	cream of mushroom soup	+	soy sauce	=	Chinese Chicken & Noodles
ham, cubed	+	broccoli, cut into flowerets	+	potatoes, diced	+	cream of broccoli soup	+	garlic powder	=	Ham & Broccoli with Potatoes
kielbasa, sliced	+	onion, chopped	+	rotini or penne pasta	+	pasta sauce	+	grated Parmesan cheese	=	Sausage-Pasta Bake
turkey, chopped	+	tomatoes, diced	+	rice	+	cream of chicken soup	+	green chiles, diced	=	South-of-the Border Turkey & Rice

Combine ingredients in a 2-quart casserole dish. Cover and bake at 350 degrees for 30 minutes or until tender. Serves 4.

Use this handy formula to stir up quick meals with what you have on hand. Just copy, cut and hang on the fridge or inside a cabinet door for easy reference!

Slow-Cooker Specials

SLOWLY SIMMERED SUPPERS

Vegetable Beef Soup

Cami Cherryholmes
Urbana, IA

This recipe is as good-tasting as it is easy...it also freezes well.

1 lb. ground beef, browned
16-oz. pkg. frozen mixed
   vegetables
12-oz. can cocktail vegetable
   juice

3 c. water
1/2 c. pearled barley
1-1/2 oz. pkg. onion soup mix
3 cubes beef bouillon

Combine all ingredients in a slow cooker; cook on low setting for 6 to 8 hours. Serves 4 to 6.

Get out your slow cooker today...there's nothing like
coming home to the aroma of dinner just waiting
to be served!

Beans & Weenies

Sharon Crider
Lebanon, MO

*A year 'round favorite...a standby for summer picnics, yet hearty
and satisfying during cold weather too!*

1-lb. pkg. wieners, quartered
3 16-oz. cans pork & beans
1/4 c. onion, chopped

1/2 c. catsup
1/4 c. molasses
2 t. mustard

Combine all ingredients in a slow cooker; cover and heat on low
setting for 3 to 4 hours. Makes 6 servings.

Attach a row of vintage glass doorknobs across a wooden
board...a handy hanging rack for coats and sweaters.

·Slow-Cooker Specials·

Southern Pork Barbecue ▶

Vicki Chavis
Fort Myers, FL

My whole family loves this recipe and my friends ask for it by name.
It's a great way to serve a picnic crowd.

3-lb. boneless pork loin roast,
   trimmed
1 c. water
18-oz. bottle barbecue sauce
2 T. Worcestershire sauce
1 to 2 T. hot pepper sauce

1/4 c. brown sugar, packed
1 t. salt
1 t. pepper
16 to 20 mini hamburger
   buns, split

Place roast in a slow cooker; add water. Cover and cook on high
setting for 7 hours. Shred meat; return to slow cooker. Stir in
remaining ingredients; cover and cook on low setting for one hour.
Serve on buns, topped with coleslaw. Makes 8 to 10 servings,
2 buns each.

Coleslaw:

1 head cabbage, shredded
3 carrots, peeled and shredded
1 c. mayonnaise

1/3 c. sugar
1/4 c. cider vinegar

Combine cabbage and carrots. Blend remaining ingredients; toss with
cabbage mixture. Makes 10 servings.

Invite new neighbors to share your next hearty slow-cooker
meal. Send them home with a gift basket filled with flyers
from favorite bakeries and pizza parlors, coupons and local
maps...tuck in a package of homemade cookies.
So thoughtful!

Easy Pork & Sauerkraut

Carrie Knotts
Kalispell, MT

So tasty! It's very easy to double for heartier appetites.

1 lb. boneless pork, cubed
32-oz. jar sauerkraut, drained
12-oz. bottle beer
1/2 apple, cored and peeled

1 T. garlic, minced
2 t. dill weed
1 t. onion salt
1 t. dry mustard

Combine all ingredients in a slow cooker; heat on high setting for one hour. Reduce heat to low setting and continue heating for 5 hours or until pork is cooked through. Discard apple before serving.
Serves 4 to 6.

No peeking! Lifting the lid of your slow cooker releases heat and can lengthen the cooking time.

Smoky Sausage Dinner

Lisa Hains
Tipp City, OH

For even simpler preparation, use canned small potatoes and cook just until everything is heated through.

6 to 8 potatoes, peeled and
  quartered
2 14-1/2 oz. cans French-style
  green beans, drained and
  juice of 1 can reserved

1 lb. smoked sausage, sliced
salt and garlic powder to taste

Arrange potatoes in a slow cooker; top with green beans and reserved juice. Arrange sausage on top; sprinkle with salt and garlic powder. Cover and heat on high setting about 6 hours or until potatoes are tender. Makes 4 to 6 servings.

Pierced tin lanterns are so pretty twinkling along the front walk. Fill an empty tin can with water, freeze solid, then tap a design of holes all around with awl and hammer. When the ice has melted, set a pillar candle inside.

Colorado Pork Chops

Linda Wolfe
Westminster, CO

These tasty pork chops feature all the flavors of your favorite Mexican restaurant. Serve with soft flour tortillas or crispy corn tortilla chips.

6 pork chops
15-oz. can chili beans with
   chili sauce
1-1/2 c. salsa

1 c. corn
Optional: green chiles to taste
3 to 4 c. prepared rice
Garnish: fresh cilantro, chopped

Layer ingredients in order given in a slow cooker, except for rice and cilantro. Heat on low setting for 5 hours or high setting for 2-1/2 hours. Serve over prepared rice; garnish with cilantro. Serves 6.

Fluffy, tender baked potatoes for a crowd…just fix & forget! Pierce 10 to 12 baking potatoes with a fork and wrap each in aluminum foil. Arrange potatoes in a slow cooker, cover and cook on high setting for 2-1/2 to 4 hours, until fork tender.

Frank's Chicken

Tricia Roberson
Indian Head, MD

The mouthwatering gravy is tasty over rice.

4 potatoes, peeled and quartered
1 carrot, peeled and chopped
1 onion, diced
1 stalk celery, chopped
6 to 8 chicken legs and thighs
1/2 c. chicken broth
1/4 c. white wine or chicken
   broth

1/2 T. paprika
2 t. garlic powder
1/2 t. dried rosemary
1/2 t. dried basil
Optional: 2 to 3 T. cornstarch

Place vegetables in bottom of slow cooker; arrange chicken on top.
Pour chicken broth and wine or additional broth over all; sprinkle with
seasonings. Heat on low setting for 8 hours or on high setting for
5 hours. Remove chicken and vegetables to a serving platter. If
desired, stir cornstarch into juices in slow cooker until thickened to
make gravy. Serves 4 to 6.

Homemade salt-free seasoning is tasty on veggies and meats.
Combine a tablespoon each of dried oregano, basil and
pepper, 1-1/2 teaspoons each onion powder and thyme and a
teaspoon of garlic powder. Fill a large shaker container to
keep conveniently by the stove.

Thai Peanut Chicken ▶

Patricia Olinik
Quebec, Canada

*I found this recipe one day when I was searching for something
new to try. It has since become one of my staple recipes,
and I always look forward to the next time I get to make it!*

3/4 c. salsa
1/4 c. creamy peanut butter
3/4 c. light coconut milk
2 T. lime juice
1 T. soy sauce
1 t. sugar
2 cloves garlic, finely chopped
2 T. fresh ginger, peeled and
　grated, or 1 T. ground ginger

2 lbs. boneless, skinless chicken
　thighs, each cut into 2 to
　3 pieces
cooked rice
Garnish: chopped peanuts,
　chopped fresh cilantro

Combine salsa, peanut butter, coconut milk, lime juice, soy sauce,
sugar, garlic and ginger in a slow cooker; mix well. Add chicken; stir
to coat. Cover and cook on low setting for 8 hours, or until chicken is
very tender and sauce has thickened. Serve over rice; garnish as
desired. Serves 4.

Watch yard sales for vintage-style glass or china items to
decorate your garden. A glass globe perched in a birdbath or
mismatched saucers bordering the flowerbed
add character to your garden.

Classic Chicken Cacciatore

Jackie Smulski
Lyons, IL

Try this rich saucy stew served over rice or thin spaghetti too.

2 T. olive oil
2 boneless, skinless chicken
    breasts, cut into strips
1/2 c. all-purpose flour
pepper to taste
1/2 c. white wine or chicken
    broth, divided
1 onion, chopped
1 green pepper, chopped
2 cloves garlic, minced
1/2 t. dried oregano
1/2 t. dried basil

2 T. fresh Italian parsley,
    chopped
2 14-oz. cans diced Italian
    tomatoes
14-oz. jar Italian pasta sauce
    with vegetables
8-oz. pkg. mushrooms, chopped
6-oz. pkg. broad egg noodles,
    cooked
Garnish: grated Parmesan
    cheese

Heat olive oil in slow cooker on high setting. Coat chicken in flour and pepper; add to slow cooker. Cover and heat for 1-1/2 to 2 hours, until chicken is no longer pink. Stir in 1/4 cup wine or broth. Add onion, green pepper, garlic and herbs; heat until onion is tender. Add tomatoes, pasta sauce and mushrooms; heat to a slow boil, about 30 minutes to one hour. Serve over cooked noodles; sprinkle with Parmesan cheese. Serves 3 to 4.

Create a cozy Italian restaurant feel for your next pasta dinner. Toss a red & white checked tablecloth over the table, light drip candles in empty bottles and add a basket of garlic bread.

Company Chicken & Stuffing

Amy Blanchard
Hazel Park, MI

Try Cheddar or brick cheese for a tasty flavor change.

4 boneless, skinless chicken
   breasts
4 slices Swiss cheese
1 pkg. chicken-flavored stuffing
   mix

2 10-3/4 oz. cans cream of
   chicken soup
1/2 c. chicken broth

Arrange chicken in slow cooker; top each piece with a slice of cheese.
Mix together stuffing mix, broth and soup; pour into slow cooker. Heat
on low setting for 6 to 8 hours. Serves 4.

Make a memory table to showcase your family's good times
together. Paint a small table, then arrange a variety of
clippings, cutouts, ticket stubs and photos on top, gluing in
place with craft glue. Apply several thin coats of decoupage
medium with a sponge brush, let dry and set a
glass top in place.

Creamy Chicken & Broccoli

Ellen Lockhart
Blacksburg, VA

Substitute frozen asparagus for the broccoli if you like.

4 boneless, skinless chicken
  breasts
10-3/4 oz. can cream of chicken
  soup
2 c. milk
pepper to taste

dried, minced onion to taste
2 to 4 slices pasteurized
  processed cheese spread,
  diced
12-oz. pkg. frozen broccoli
3 to 4 c. prepared rice

Arrange chicken in slow cooker. Combine soup, milk, pepper, onion and cheese; pour over chicken. Heat on low setting for 7 hours. Add frozen broccoli; increase heat to high setting and heat for one hour until broccoli is crisp-tender. Serve over prepared rice. Makes 4 servings.

Welcome a special overnight guest with a few thoughtful touches in your guest room. A cozy fleece throw on the bed, a basket of sweet-scented toiletries, a stack of books and a night light all say "We're glad to have you!"

Cheesy Chicken & Potatoes

Barbara Cordle
London, OH

I often use my slow cooker at a cabin in Ohio's beautiful Hocking Hills...it allows me to spend more time relaxing with my family. They ask for this recipe every time we go!

32-oz. pkg. frozen hashbrowns
16-oz. pkg. frozen broccoli
2 10-3/4 oz. cans Cheddar
  cheese soup
2 12-oz. cans evaporated milk
1-1/2 lbs. boneless, skinless
  chicken breasts, cubed

6-oz. can French fried onions,
  divided
salt and pepper to taste
12-oz. pkg. shredded Cheddar
  cheese

Combine hashbrowns, broccoli, soup, milk, chicken and half the onions in a slow cooker sprayed with non-stick vegetable spray. Add salt and pepper to taste; stir and cover. Heat on low setting for 8 to 9 hours or on high setting for 4 hours. Stir in shredded cheese during the last 30 minutes of heating time. Sprinkle with remaining onions before serving. Serves 6 to 8.

Look for distinctive platters, bowls or even a whole set of special dishes to use on holidays and birthdays with your family. Years from now, your children and grandchildren will cherish these dishes for the memories they bring back.

Lillian's Beef Stew

Nancy Dynes
Goose Creek, SC

My mother made this for us when we were small children and now I make it for my own family. It's a wonderful dinner to come home to on a cold day.

2 lbs. stew beef, cubed
2 potatoes, peeled and quartered
3 stalks celery, diced
4 carrots, peeled and thickly
    sliced
2 onions, quartered
2 c. cocktail vegetable juice

1/3 c. quick-cooking tapioca,
    uncooked
1 T. sugar
1 T. salt
1/2 t. dried basil
1/4 t. pepper

Arrange beef and vegetables in slow cooker. Combine remaining ingredients; pour into slow cooker. Cover and heat on low setting for 8 to 10 hours. Serves 8.

Stir up a loaf of beer bread for dinner. Combine 3 cups self-rising flour, a 12-ounce can of beer and 3 tablespoons sugar in a greased loaf pan. Bake for 25 minutes at 350 degrees, then drizzle with melted butter. Fragrant and tasty!

Black Bean Chili ▶

Darrell Lawry
Kissimmee, FL

A different kind of chili! I like to top the bowl with
a handful of crushed tortilla chips.

1-lb. pork tenderloin
3 15-1/2 oz. cans black beans,
    drained and rinsed
16-oz. jar chunky salsa
1/2 c. chicken broth
1 green pepper, chopped

1 onion, chopped
2 t. chili powder
1 t. ground cumin
1 t. dried oregano
Garnish: sour cream, diced
    tomatoes

Place pork in a lightly greased slow cooker; add remaining ingredients
except garnish. Cover and cook on low setting for 8 hours, or on high
setting for 4 hours. Shred pork; return to slow cooker. Garnish
servings with dollops of sour cream and diced tomatoes. Serves 4 to 6.

Next to jazz music, there is nothing that lifts
the spirits and strengthens the soul more than
a good bowl of chili.
-Harry James

Hamburger Soup

Barbara Pache
Marshall, WI

It's wonderful to come home and find this scrumptious soup waiting for you!

1 lb. ground beef, browned and
   drained
28-oz. can crushed tomatoes
1 c. potatoes, peeled and diced
1 c. carrots, peeled and chopped
1 c. onion, sliced
1 c. celery, sliced

4 c. hot water
1 T. salt
1/2 t. pepper
1/2 t. dried basil
1/2 t. dried thyme
1 bay leaf, crumbled

Mix together all ingredients in a slow cooker. Heat on low setting for 6 to 8 hours or until vegetables are tender. Serves 4 to 6.

Cherished family photos are too precious to hide away in albums. Choose the best...the sweetest, most memorable or amusing, and have enlargements made. Framed in groups, they'll make you smile every day.

Spanish Rice

Sharon Crider
Lebanon, MO

Corn chips are tasty for scooping up this delicious dish.

2 lbs. ground beef, browned and
  drained
28-oz. can crushed tomatoes
8-oz. can tomato sauce
2 green peppers, chopped
2 onions, chopped

1 c. water
2-1/2 t. chili powder
2 t. Worcestershire sauce
2 t. salt
1 c. long-cooking rice, uncooked

Combine all ingredients in a slow cooker; mix well. Cover and heat on low setting for 6 to 8 hours or on high setting for 3-1/2 hours. Serves 8 to 10.

Give your fireplace a welcoming autumn glow...fill it with pots of flame-colored orange and yellow marigolds or mums.

Slow-Cooker Fajitas

Erin Gumm
Omaha, NE

These are always a favorite for casual dinner parties or when the whole family gets together...and the slow cooker does all the work!

1-1/2 lbs. beef round steak
8-oz. can diced tomatoes,
   drained
1 onion, sliced
1 green pepper, cut into strips
1 red pepper, cut into strips
1 jalapeño, chopped
1 t. fresh cilantro, chopped
2 cloves garlic, minced

1 t. chili powder
1 t. ground cumin
1 t. ground coriander
1/4 t. salt
8 to 10 flour tortillas
Garnish: sour cream, guacamole,
   salsa, shredded cheese,
   shredded lettuce

Place steak in bottom of a slow cooker. Combine vegetables and seasonings; spoon over steak. Cover and heat on low setting for 8 to 10 hours or on high setting for 4 to 5 hours. Shred meat; serve with a slotted spoon on tortillas and garnish with favorite toppings. Serves 8 to 10.

A tray of warm, moistened towels will be welcomed by your guests after a meal of finger foods. Soak fingertip towels in water and a bit of lemon juice, roll up and microwave on high for 10 to 15 seconds.

Slow-Cooker Enchiladas

Laura Harp
Bolivar, MO

Cheesy and easy! Serve with tortilla chips.

1 lb. ground beef, browned and
  drained
1/2 c. onion, chopped
10-oz. can enchilada sauce
10-3/4 oz. can nacho cheese
  soup
10-3/4 oz. can cream of
  mushroom soup

15-oz. can corn, drained
16-oz. can pinto beans, drained
  and rinsed
1/2 c. sliced black olives
4 corn tortillas
2 c. shredded Cheddar cheese,
  divided

Combine all ingredients except tortillas and shredded cheese. Place
one tortilla in the bottom of a slow cooker; spoon one-quarter of the
beef mixture over tortilla, followed by 1/2 cup of cheese. Repeat layers
until all ingredients are used, ending with cheese. Heat on high setting
for one hour until cheese is melted and bubbling. Serves 6 to 8.

Scrapbooking is a great family activity. Let the kids help
if they're old enough to handle scissors and glue, and the
results will be even more precious. Use 3-ring binder
albums...more flexible than bound scrapbooks,
since pages can be added or rearranged.

Potato-Corn Chowder

Jerry Bostian
Oelwein, IA

Short on time? Use a package of ready-cooked bacon instead.

2 10-3/4 oz. cans potato soup
2 14-3/4 oz. cans cream-style
    corn
8 slices bacon, crisply cooked
    and crumbled
Optional: 1 to 2 T. bacon
    drippings

1/2 to 1 c. milk
salt, pepper and garlic salt
    to taste
Garnish: fresh parsley, chopped

Blend soup and corn in a slow cooker; add bacon along with bacon drippings, if desired. Add milk until soup is of desired consistency; add salt, pepper and garlic salt to taste. Heat on low setting for 8 to 10 hours. Sprinkle individual servings with parsley. Serves 6 to 8.

Chowders and cream soups are perfect comfort foods. Make yours extra creamy and rich tasting…simply replace milk or water in the recipe with an equal amount of evaporated milk.

Reid Family Pork Chops

Marsha Reid
Pasadena, CA

My family loves these chops with their savory combination of flavors.

4 to 6 boneless pork chops
salt and pepper to taste
2 onions, chopped
2 stalks celery, chopped
1 green pepper, sliced
14-1/2 oz. can stewed tomatoes
1/2 c. catsup
2 T. cider vinegar

2 T. brown sugar
2 T. Worcestershire sauce
1 T. lemon juice
1 cube beef bouillon
2 T. cornstarch
2 T. water
2 to 3 c. prepared rice

Season pork chops with salt and pepper; arrange in slow cooker. Add onions, celery, green pepper and tomatoes. Combine catsup, vinegar, sugar, Worcestershire sauce, lemon juice and bouillon cube; pour over vegetables. Cover and heat on low setting for 5 to 6 hours. Mix together cornstarch and water until smooth; pour into slow cooker. Cover and heat on high setting for 30 minutes until thickened. Serve over prepared rice. Makes 4 to 6 servings.

Grandma's vintage cookie cutters, whisk, potato masher and other kitchen utensils make a nostalgic display in your kitchen when arranged on a grapevine wreath with raffia ties.

Bacon & Wild Rice Soup

Judy Sellgren
Wyoming, MI

This smells great when I come home after a long day
of work or shopping!

1 lb. bacon, crisply cooked and
    crumbled
1 c. celery, chopped
1 onion, diced
12-oz. pkg. sliced mushrooms
1 c. prepared instant wild rice

2 10-3/4 oz. cans cream
    of mushroom soup
2 10-3/4 oz. cans cream
    of chicken soup
2 c. water
2 c. half-and-half

Combine all ingredients except half-and-half in slow cooker. Heat on low setting for 8 to 10 hours or on high setting for 4 to 6 hours. Stir in half-and-half 30 minutes before end of heating time. Serves 8.

Invite your friends to a Soup Supper potluck in cool weather. Line up slow cookers filled with hearty soups, plus one for hot cider and one for a fruit cobbler. A basket of breads completes the menu. Add a stack of bandannas for colorful napkins.

Souped-Up Clam Chowder

Cheri Emery
Quincy, IL

We love crunchy oyster crackers with this creamy chowder.

3 10-3/4 oz. cans clam chowder
2 10-3/4 oz. cans cream of
    celery soup
10-3/4 oz. can cream of onion
    soup

2 6-1/2 oz. cans minced clams
4 c. half-and-half
1/2 c. butter

Combine all ingredients in slow cooker; heat on low setting for
6 hours. Serves 10 to 12.

Make a sweet potpourri jar. Preserve petals from flower
bouquets by spreading on a paper towel until dry. Add garden
flowers and herb leaves as available, sprinkling with a few
drops of scented oil. Once the jar is full, leave open
to enjoy the scent.

The Best Pot Roast Ever

Joan Brochu
Hardwick, VT

This roast cooks up so tender…you'll love the gravy too.

2 c. water
5 to 6-lb. beef pot roast
1-oz. pkg. ranch salad dressing
   mix
.7-oz. pkg. Italian salad
   dressing mix

.87-oz. pkg. brown gravy mix
6 to 8 potatoes, peeled and
   cubed
8 to 10 carrots, peeled and
   thickly sliced

Pour water into slow cooker; add roast. Combine mixes and sprinkle over roast. Heat on low setting for 6 to 7 hours; add potatoes and carrots during the last 2 hours. Serves 6 to 8.

I have 3 chairs in my house: one for solitude,
2 for friendship, 3 for company.
-Henry David Thoreau

Slow-Cooker Swiss Steak

Lisa Ludwig
Fort Wayne, IN

Your family will love this flavorful version of an old favorite. Pick up a container of heat & eat mashed potatoes for an easy side.

2-lb. beef chuck roast, cut into
    serving-size pieces
3/4 c. all-purpose flour, divided
2 to 3 T. oil
16-oz. can diced tomatoes

1 onion, sliced
1 stalk celery, sliced
1 T. browning and seasoning
    sauce

Coat beef with 1/2 cup flour; sauté in oil in a skillet until browned. Arrange beef in a slow cooker. Combine remaining ingredients except remaining flour and pour over beef; heat on low setting for 6 to 8 hours. Slowly stir in remaining flour to make gravy, adding water if necessary. Heat on high setting for 15 minutes, until thickened. Serves 4.

Fill the base of a large hurricane lamp with pretty beach pebbles or colored glass gems, then top with a fat pillar candle for a delightful centerpiece.

·Slow-Cooker Specials·

1-2-3 Tomato-Onion Roast

Jacqueline Kurtz
Reading, PA

This is so delicious, you won't believe how simple it is!

3 to 4-lb. beef chuck roast
1-1/2 oz. pkg. onion soup mix

14-1/2 oz. can stewed tomatoes

Place roast in slow cooker; top with soup mix and tomatoes. Cover and heat on low for 8 hours. Serves 6 to 8.

Rainy day fun! Make cereal necklaces with the kids by stringing together fruit-flavored ring-shaped cereal...instant beads that are perfectly safe for nibbling.

Easy Slow-Cooker Beef Stew

Christy Neubert
O'Fallon, IL

My sister, Crystal, gave me this wonderful recipe. It's so yummy and easy, all you need is fruit and warm bread to make a meal.

1-1/2 lbs. stew beef, cubed
8-oz. pkg. baby carrots
3 to 4 potatoes, cubed
10-3/4 oz. can tomato soup
10-3/4 oz. can beef broth
10-3/4 oz. can French onion soup

Place beef in bottom of a slow cooker sprayed with non-stick vegetable spray. Arrange carrots and potatoes over beef. Combine soups and pour over vegetables. Cover; heat on low setting for 8 to 10 hours or high setting for 6 hours. Serves 3 to 4.

Clear plastic over-the-door shoe holders provide handy storage for craft materials or sewing supplies...they hang in unused space and let you see what's inside. They're great for organizing kids' stuff too!

Fire & Spice Baked Ham

Linda Belon
Steubenville, OH

*Is there anything more taste-tempting than the aroma of
a baked ham? We don't think so!*

5-1/2 to 6-lb. fully-cooked ham
   half
1/2 c. red pepper jelly

1/2 c. pineapple preserves
1/4 c. brown sugar, packed
1/4 t. ground cloves

Trim off rind and excess fat from ham; score fat in a diamond pattern.
Place ham on a broiler pan sprayed with non-stick vegetable spray.
Combine remaining ingredients in a small saucepan over low heat,
stirring with a whisk until well blended. Brush 1/3 of jelly mixture over
ham. Bake, uncovered, at 425 degrees for 5 minutes. Turn down oven
temperature to 325 degrees. Bake ham for an additional 45 minutes,
basting with remaining jelly mixture every 15 minutes. Transfer ham
to a serving platter; let stand for 15 minutes before slicing. Makes 8 to
10 servings.

An old frame makes a quaint tea tray. Spray it white, then
arrange snippets of vintage Valentines, Christmas cards or
postcards underneath the glass. Add embroidered linens or
bits of lace as accents.

Sausage-Sauerkraut Supper

Jen Burnham
Delaware, OH

The flavors of Oktoberfest in a single dish!

4 c. carrots, peeled and
   thickly sliced
4 c. potatoes, quartered
2 14-oz. cans sauerkraut,
   drained and rinsed
2-1/2 lbs. Polish sausage,
   browned and cut into 3-inch
   pieces

1 onion, diced
3 cloves garlic, minced
1-1/2 c. dry white wine
   or chicken broth
1 t. pepper
1/2 t. caraway seed

Layer carrots, potatoes, sauerkraut and sausage in a slow cooker.
Combine onion, garlic, wine or broth, pepper and caraway seed; pour
over sausage. Cover and heat on low setting for 8 to 9 hours or until
vegetables are tender and sausage is no longer pink. Serves 10 to 12.

Need a centerpiece in a jiffy? Simply arrange slices of orange,
lemon or lime inside a tall clear glass jar, fill with water and
light a floating candle on top.

·Slow-Cooker Specials·

Fix & Forget Stuffed Peppers

Beth Kramer
Port Saint Lucie, FL

Use red or yellow peppers for bright color and a milder taste.

1 lb. ground beef
1 c. long-cooking rice, uncooked
1 onion, chopped
1 carrot, peeled and shredded
1 t. beef bouillon granules

1/2 t. salt
1/2 t. pepper
6 green peppers, tops removed
10-3/4 oz. can tomato soup
1-1/4 c. water

Combine ground beef, rice, onion, carrot, bouillon, salt and pepper; stuff each pepper about 2/3 full. Arrange peppers side-by-side in slow cooker. Combine soup and water; pour over peppers. Cover and heat on low setting for 6 to 8 hours. Makes 6 servings.

Bring a treasured family quilt out of hiding.
To hang it safely, stitch a fabric sleeve to the back of the top edge, then slip a decorative curtain rod through. Hang the quilt away from strong sunlight...your family and guests will enjoy it for many years to come.

Stewed Black-Eyed Peas

Leslie Stimel
Westerville, OH

Andouille is a spicy sausage from Louisiana. Substitute another spicy smoked sausage if you like.

1 lb. dried black-eyed peas
1 lb. andouille sausage, cut into
   1/4-inch slices
1 c. yellow onion, chopped
1/2 t. salt
2 T. hot pepper sauce

5 cloves garlic, pressed
4 bay leaves
1 t. dried thyme
1 t. dried parsley
8 c. chicken broth

Combine all ingredients in a slow cooker; heat on low setting for 5 to 6 hours. Discard bay leaves. Serves 8 to 10.

Create a whimsical mosaic pot with bits of broken china and tile. Arrange pieces in a pleasing design and glue to a terra cotta pot with tile adhesive. When dry, mix up some tile grout and apply it all over, pressing grout between the glued-on pieces. Wipe off excess grout with a damp cloth.

Pepperoni-Pizza Rigatoni

Jo Ann

Personalize this recipe by adding mushrooms, black olives or any of your family's other favorite pizza toppings.

1-1/2 lbs. ground beef, browned
8-oz. pkg. rigatoni, cooked
16-oz. pkg. shredded mozzarella
   cheese

10-3/4 oz. can cream of tomato
   soup
2 14-oz. jars pizza sauce
8-oz. pkg. sliced pepperoni

Alternate layers of ground beef, cooked rigatoni, cheese, soup, sauce and pepperoni in a slow cooker. Heat on low setting for 4 hours. Serves 6.

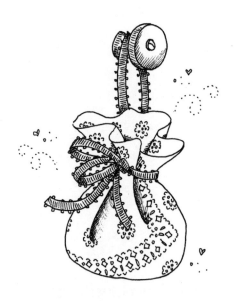

A sweet-smelling home is a cozy home. Wrap dried lavender or rose petals in lace hankies and tie with satin ribbon to tuck into dresser drawers and hang from drawer pulls.

Spaghetti for a Crowd

Regina Vining
Warwick, RI

*After cooking all day, the flavor is tremendous! There's no added oil,
so this sauce is low-fat too.*

5 29-oz. cans tomato sauce
3 6-oz. cans tomato paste
3 cloves garlic, minced
1 onion, chopped
3 T. dried rosemary
3 T. dried oregano
3 T. dried thyme

3 T. dried parsley
1 bay leaf
1/8 t. red pepper flakes
8 to 10 c. prepared spaghetti
Garnish: grated Parmesan
  cheese

Combine all ingredients except spaghetti and Parmesan cheese in slow
cooker. Heat on high setting for 3 to 4 hours, stirring frequently.
Discard bay leaf. Serve over prepared spaghetti, sprinkled with
Parmesan. Serves 6 to 10.

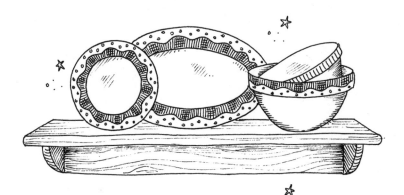

Visit a paint-your-own pottery studio to create one platter or a
whole set of dishes for your family. Better yet, take your
children along. They will beam with pride when they see
"their" dishes on the dinner table!

Slow-Cooker Dinner Math

Toss ingredients into your slow cooker for a dinner that cooks itself...even makes its own gravy!

Meat	+ Veggies	+ Starch	+ Sauce	+ Add-Ins	= Your Dinner
1 to 2 lbs., uncooked	1-1/2 to 2 c. fresh, or canned	2 c.	2 cans or 2 c.	one or more to taste	
boneless, skinless chicken breasts	salsa or tomatoes and green chiles, diced	instant rice (stir in 20 mins. before end of cooking time)	tomato, cream of, or chicken soups	shredded cheese (stir in after cooking is done)	Chicken Enchilada Stew
beef chuck, cut into strips	mushrooms, sliced	cooked egg noodles (add after cooking is done)	cream of mushroom soup	sour cream (stir in after cooking is done)	Beef Stroganoff
boneless pork ribs, cut into serving-size pieces	onions, sliced	navy or baked beans	barbecue sauce	tomatoes, diced	BBQ Pork & Beans
kielbasa, halved	sauerkraut	frozen shredded hashbrowns	French onion soup	onion soup mix (add with canned soup)	Sausage & Sauerkraut Supper
beef chuck roast	carrots and onions, quartered	potatoes, quartered	golden mushroom soup	Worcestershire sauce	Beef Stew

Arrange vegetables in bottom of slow cooker; arrange meat on top. Top with soup or sauce and sprinkle with add-ins. Cook on low setting for 8 to 10 hours or high setting for 4 to 5 hours. Makes 4 servings.

Use this handy formula to stir up quick meals with what you have on hand. Just copy, cut and hang on the fridge or inside a cabinet door for easy reference!

Microwave Magic

COUNTERTOP COOKING

Microwave Magic

Layered Ham & Asparagus Strata

Tiffany Brinkley
Broomfield, CO

A good make-ahead dish...assemble and refrigerate the night before, then cook in the microwave at serving time.

12 to 16 thick slices Italian
  bread
1 c. shredded mozzarella cheese,
  divided
1 c. cooked ham, diced and
  divided

2 c. asparagus, chopped and
  divided
6 eggs
1 c. milk
2 T. lemon juice
1/4 t. garlic powder

Spray an 8"x8" microwave-safe baking dish with non-stick vegetable spray. Arrange half of bread in dish; sprinkle with half each of cheese, ham and asparagus. Repeat layering with remaining cheese, ham and asparagus. Blend together remaining ingredients; pour over top. Cover with plastic wrap; microwave on high for 5 minutes. Rotate dish 1/4 turn; microwave on medium for an additional 10 to 12 minutes, rotating dish occasionally, until knife inserted at center comes out clean. Serves 4 to 6.

Microwaves can do lots more than pop popcorn! Meats, fruit and veggies cook in just 6 minutes per pound in a full-size microwave oven on high power. Fish and seafood take 3 to 4 minutes per pound. After cooking, let food stand, covered, for a few minutes more.

Garden-Fresh Gazpacho, page 166

Sandra's Pomegranate
Salad, page 179

French Onion Soup, page 26

Goalpost Apple Slaw, page 176

Pizza Pasta Salad, page 164

Fiesta Bubble Bread, page 50

Marvelous Minestrone, page 22

Mac & Cheese Cupcakes, page 57

Herbed Mashed Potatoes, page 19

Deep South Chicken & Dumplings, page 7

Ham & Swiss [...] ge 48

Golden Parmesan Roasted Potatoes,
page 49

Southern Pork BBQ Sandwich, page 80

Deep-Dish Skillet Pizza, page 55

Jo Ann's Garden Frittata, page 18

Thai Peanut Chicken, page 85

Big Eddie's Rigatoni, page 67

Black Bean Chili, page 91

Easy Bacon Frittata, page 8

Peanut Butter Texas Sheet Cake, page 197

Crustless Pumpkin Pie, page 207

Fire & Spice Baked Ham, page 104

Sweet Hummingbird Cake, page 211

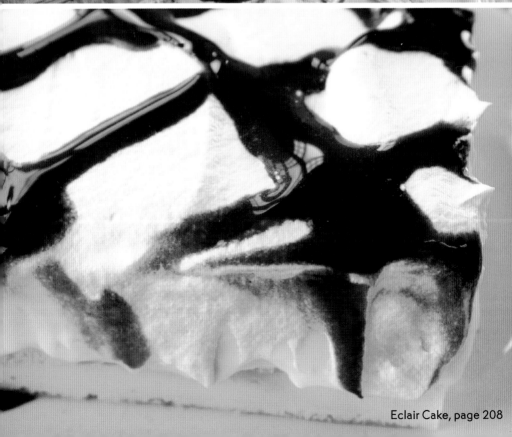
Eclair Cake, page 208

Jenn's Pistachio-Cranberry
Cookies, page 184

Sweet Ambrosia Salad, page 216

Ham Frittata

Irene Robinson
Cincinnati, OH

My family loves this quick, filling dish for brunch or dinner. It's a great way to use up leftover ham.

1 T. butter
1 c. cooked ham, diced
1/2 c. onion, chopped

1/4 c. green pepper, chopped
4 eggs, beaten
salt and pepper to taste

Melt butter in a microwave-safe bowl; add ham, onion and green pepper. Cover; microwave on high for 2 minutes. Stir in eggs, salt and pepper; microwave on high for an additional 1-1/2 to 2-1/2 minutes. Let stand 3 minutes or until completely set. Serves 2 to 4.

We love breakfast foods, but it seems like there's never time to linger over them in the morning. Enjoy an unhurried breakfast with your family...at dinnertime! Ham Frittata is perfect. Just add a basket of muffins, fresh fruit and a steamy pot of tea.

Mediterranean Chicken & Rice

Vickie

A delightful change from creamy chicken & rice...give it a try!

1 T. oil
1 onion, chopped
1 c. green pepper, chopped
2 c. instant rice, uncooked
1-3/4 c. tomato juice
1 c. frozen peas

1/3 c. olives with pimentos,
   chopped
1/2 t. salt
1/8 t. pepper
2-1/2 to 3 lbs. chicken
1/2 t. paprika

Combine oil, onion and green pepper in a 13"x9" microwave-safe dish. Microwave on high for 3-1/2 minutes. Stir in rice, tomato juice, peas, olives, salt and pepper. Arrange chicken on top, with the meatiest sides facing outer edges of dish. Cover with plastic wrap; microwave on high 10 minutes. Turn chicken over; rotate dish and sprinkle with paprika. Recover; microwave on high an additional 7 to 10 minutes until chicken and rice are tender. Serves 4 to 6.

Start a family tradition...have a candlelight dinner once a week with your children. Lit tapers, snowy-white napkins and the best china will let your kids know they are special. They'll be on their best behavior too.

Easy Chicken Dinner

Geneva Rogers
Gillette, WY

We love this cheesy, crunchy way to serve chicken.

2 T. butter
6 boneless, skinless chicken
    breasts
1 t. salt
1 t. pepper

8-oz. can sliced mushrooms,
    drained
8-oz. can French fried onions
1/2 c. shredded Monterey Jack
    cheese

Melt butter in a 13"x9" microwave-safe baking dish. Arrange chicken in dish. Turn to coat with butter; sprinkle with salt and pepper. Cover; microwave on high for 5 minutes. Turn chicken over; top with mushrooms and microwave an additional 5 minutes until chicken is no longer pink. Top with onions and cheese; microwave, uncovered, one to 2 minutes until cheese melts. Serves 6.

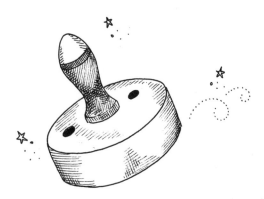

Perk up plain biscuits with honey-pecan butter. Simply blend together 1/2 cup butter, 1/2 cup honey and 1/3 cup toasted chopped pecans. Yummy!

Beef with Peppers & Tomatoes

Audrey Lett
Newark, DE

A Chinese restaurant favorite...serve over chow mein noodles instead of rice for a crunchy change.

1 lb. beef flank steak, thinly
    sliced across the grain
1/3 c. soy sauce
1/3 c. red wine or beef broth
1 t. sugar
2 T. cornstarch

1 onion, sliced
2 c. sliced mushrooms
1 green pepper, cut in strips
1 pt. cherry tomatoes, halved
2 to 3 c. prepared rice

Arrange steak in a 2-quart microwave-safe baking dish. Combine soy sauce, wine or broth and sugar; pour over meat and mix lightly to coat evenly. Refrigerate one to 2 hours. Stir in cornstarch, onion, mushrooms and green pepper. Cover; heat in microwave on high for 7 to 9 minutes or until sauce is thickened. Stir halfway through cooking time. Add tomatoes; cover and heat for one additional minute or until heated through. Serve over prepared rice. Serves 5.

Freshen up yard sale baskets for handy storage. Spray with craft paint, then use a sponge or a dry brush to add accents in a second color. Tie on a big homespun bow and they're ready to hold craft supplies, bath towels or magazines around the house.

Beef Burgundy

Dana Cunningham
Lafayette, LA

Toss egg noodles with butter and parsley for the perfect partner to this dish.

4 slices bacon
2 T. plus 2 t. all-purpose flour
1 t. beef bouillon granules
1/2 t. dried basil
1 lb. stew beef, cubed

14-1/2 oz. can diced tomatoes
1/2 c. red wine or beef broth
1 c. frozen pearl onions
16 mushrooms, halved

Cover and cook bacon in a 2-quart microwave-safe baking dish on high for 2 to 2-1/2 minutes or until crisp. Drain bacon, reserving drippings in baking dish; crumble bacon and set aside. Stir flour, bouillon and basil into drippings. Add beef, tomatoes and wine or broth; mix well. Cover and microwave on high heat for 2 minutes. Continue heating on medium heat for 15 minutes, stirring twice. Stir in onions and mushrooms. Cover and microwave on medium heat for an additional 12 to 18 minutes or until meat and vegetables are tender, stirring twice. Sprinkle with reserved bacon before serving. Serves 4.

Did you know? The flavors of herbs and spices are more intense in microwaved foods. Reduce the amount you use by about 25% if you're adapting a recipe for microwave use.

Lemony Shrimp & Ravioli

Robin Hill
Rochester, NY

A delightful dinner for 2...hard to believe it's so easy to make!

1 T. butter
1/2 t. lemon zest
1/2 t. dried basil
1 T. lemon juice

9-oz. pkg. cheese ravioli, cooked
1/2 lb. raw shrimp, peeled and
   cleaned

Combine butter, lemon zest and basil in a 1-1/2 quart microwave-safe baking dish. Microwave on high for 45 seconds to one minute or until butter is melted. Add lemon juice; mix well. Add ravioli and shrimp; toss to coat and cover with parchment paper. Microwave on high, stirring once, for 3 to 4 minutes or until shrimp are opaque in center. Serves 2.

Revive the tradition of little sleep pillows to assure peaceful rest. Stitch together 2 flowered hankies on 3 sides and fill with dried herbs like chamomile, dill, lavender and peppermint. Stitch closed and tuck into your pillowcase for sweet dreams.

Madelon's Tuna & Noodles

Kristen Simon
Chicago, IL

Just as quick as a packaged dinner mix...but a lot more flavorful!

2 6 oz. cans tuna, drained
10-3/4 oz. can cream of celery
    soup
2 T. mayonnaise
3 c. prepared elbow macaroni

1/8 t. dried oregano
1/8 t. dill weed
Optional: 1/4 c. onion, chopped
6 slices American cheese

Combine all ingredients except cheese in a microwave safe bowl; mix well. Arrange cheese over all; microwave on high for 2 to 3 minutes or until heated through and cheese is melted. Serves 2 to 4.

Make time for a craft you've always wanted to learn! Grab a friend and find a class...stencil a basket, cross-stitch a pillow, quilt a table runner or knit a scarf. You'll be so glad you did!

South-of-the-Border Beef & Beans

Dale Duncan
Waterloo, IA

Serve with tortilla chips for scooping.

1 lb. ground beef
1/4 c. onion, chopped
1/4 t. salt
1/2 t. chili powder

15-1/2 oz. can kidney beans,
   drained and rinsed
10-oz. can enchilada sauce
1 c. shredded Cheddar cheese

Crumble ground beef in a 2-quart microwave-safe casserole dish. Stir in onion; cover and microwave on high for 6 minutes, until ground beef is browned. Drain; stir in remaining ingredients except cheese. Microwave on high an additional 12 to 14 minutes; sprinkle with cheese. Let stand, covered, for 5 minutes or until cheese melts. Serves 4 to 6.

Plant a butterfly garden. Your local nursery can help you select butterfly-friendly plants like Black-Eyed Susans, purple coneflower, zinnia and butterfly bush. Butterflies need a drink, so add a shallow dish of water too.

Chili-Beef Enchiladas

April Jacobs
Loveland, CO

Your kids will love this cheesy dish! Try Mexican-blend shredded cheese for extra flavor.

1/2 lb. ground beef
10-3/4 oz. can chili-beef soup, divided
1/4 c. catsup
2 T. onion, chopped
1/2 t. garlic powder

1/4 t. chili powder
1/8 t. ground cumin
8 corn tortillas
1/2 c. shredded Cheddar cheese, divided
1/2 c. water

Combine ground beef, 1/4 cup soup, catsup, onion and spices in a one-quart glass measuring cup. Microwave on high for 5 minutes, stirring once to separate beef; set aside. Wrap 2 tortillas in a damp paper towel; microwave for 40 seconds. Immediately spoon beef mixture onto both tortillas; top with one tablespoon of cheese. Roll up tightly; place seam-side down in a 1-1/2 quart shallow glass dish. Repeat until all tortillas are filled. Mix remaining soup and water; pour over enchiladas. Microwave 10 to 12 minutes or until hot, turning dish 1/2 turn every 4 minutes. Serves 4.

Bring out your favorite collectibles to be enjoyed by all.
March a collection of antique clocks, milk glass vases or
other items dear to you across a mantel.

Cheesy Chile Casserole

Kimberlee Tuttle
Elk Ridge, UT

This egg-based dish makes a tasty breakfast too...simply spoon it into flour tortillas and roll up.

5 eggs, beaten
1 c. shredded Pepper Jack cheese
1 c. shredded sharp Cheddar
   cheese
1 c. cottage cheese, drained

8-oz. can chopped green chiles,
   drained
1/4 c. all-purpose flour
1/2 t. baking powder

Mix all ingredients together well; pour into a 10"x10" microwave-safe baking dish. Microwave, uncovered, on medium-high for 12 to 15 minutes; let stand for 10 minutes. Serves 4 to 6.

Create a cozy reading corner. A comfy chair with a fleece throw, a reading lamp and a small table to hold a snack and a cup of tea will encourage your family to check out books and magazines that you've placed on a nearby shelf.

Salsa Chicken

Cathy Hillier
Salt Lake City, UT

Choose hot & spicy salsa and a few drops of hot pepper sauce if you dare!

2 T. all-purpose flour
16-oz. jar chunky-style salsa
4 boneless, skinless chicken
   breast halves

1 green pepper, sliced in rings

Shake flour in a large oven bag; place in a 13"x9" microwave-safe baking dish. Add salsa to bag; squeeze to blend with flour. Add chicken to bag; turn to coat chicken with sauce. Arrange chicken in bag with meaty sides toward outside of bag. Lay pepper rings over chicken. Close bag with nylon tie provided; cut six, 1/2-inch slits in top of bag. Microwave for 5 minutes on high; rotate dish and microwave an additional 5 to 7 minutes, until chicken is tender and juices run clear. Let stand in bag 5 minutes before serving. Serves 4.

Make your microwave citrusy fresh. Fill a microwave-safe cup with one cup water and 1/4 cup lemon juice. Heat on high for 3 minutes and simply wipe down the inside of the microwave using a soft damp cloth.

Stuffed Peppers

Debbie Dzurilla
Bartlett, IL

My mother shared this easy recipe for stuffed peppers with me.
I make it often with peppers grown in our garden.

1 lb. ground beef
1/2 c. instant rice, uncooked
1 egg, beaten
1 onion, chopped
15-oz. can tomato sauce, divided
1/2 c. catsup
1 T. Worcestershire sauce

1 t. salt
1/4 t. pepper
3 green peppers, halved
  lengthwise
1/3 c. water
1 T. sugar

Mix together ground beef, rice, egg, onion, 1/2 cup tomato sauce, catsup, Worcestershire sauce, salt and pepper; set aside. Arrange pepper halves in a large microwave-safe dish; fill with beef mixture. Combine remaining tomato sauce, water and sugar; pour over peppers. Cover dish with plastic wrap. Microwave on medium high for 20 to 25 minutes, until beef is no longer pink and peppers are tender. Serves 3 to 6.

Ah! There is nothing like staying at home
for real comfort.
-Jane Austen

Sausage-Pepper Bake

Jackie Kelley
Spencerport, NY

Substitute your favorite flavor of pasta sauce if you prefer.

1 lb. Italian sausage, casing
   removed
1 c. instant rice, uncooked
26-oz. jar sausage and fennel
   pasta sauce
1 egg

1/3 c. onion, chopped
2 T. fresh oregano, chopped
3 green peppers, halved
   lengthwise
1/2 c. grated Romano cheese

Mix sausage, rice, pasta sauce, egg, onion and oregano; stuff mixture into peppers. Place pepper halves in a microwave safe dish; pour remaining sauce over top. Cover; microwave on high for 20 minutes. Uncover; sprinkle with cheese. Serves 3 to 6.

Make name frames to show off family photos. Paint a simple frame with acrylic craft paint, then use craft glue to arrange alphabet magnets on the frame. Spell out your child's name or fun phrases with the magnets…"Baby Face" or "Smile!" Sweet and so easy a child can do it!

Microwave Magic

American Chop Suey

Wendy Zachariewicz
Meriden, CT

A New England tradition...kids love it!

1-1/2 lbs. ground beef
1 T. dried, minced onion
1 t. Italian seasoning
1 t. garlic, chopped

14-1/2 oz. can diced tomatoes
10-3/4 oz. can tomato soup
1/2 c. grated Parmesan cheese
2 c. prepared egg noodles

Combine ground beef, onion, Italian seasoning and garlic in a microwave-safe bowl. Microwave on high heat for 5 minutes, stirring frequently. Drain. Add tomatoes, soup and Parmesan cheese; microwave an additional 10 minutes. Stir in noodles; microwave for 15 minutes on medium heat or until heated through. Serves 6.

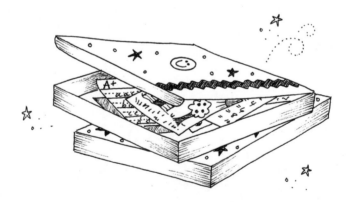

Ask your neighborhood pizzeria for an unused pizza box that you can turn into a keeping box for your child's artwork and other special papers. He or she can decorate the lid with colorful paper cut-outs, stickers and embellishments.

Fettuccine Alfredo

Kathy Grashoff
Fort Wayne, IN

We don't know who Alfredo was, but his noodles sure are tasty!

4 T. butter
3 T. all-purpose flour
2 c. milk
1/8 t. cayenne pepper
1/4 t. salt

1/8 t. white pepper
1-1/2 c. grated Parmesan
    cheese, divided
12-oz. pkg. fettuccine, cooked

In a 2-quart glass bowl, heat butter on high one minute. Stir in flour and blend well. Stir in milk, cayenne pepper, salt and white pepper. Heat on high 4 to 5 minutes or until thickened, stirring twice. Stir in one cup Parmesan cheese until melted. Toss with pasta; sprinkle with remaining cheese. Serves 4.

Decorate your dining room table with a simple table runner for each season. There are so many charming seasonal print fabrics available! You'll just need a couple of yards of fabric for a runner. Rick-rack edging and a tassel at each end are nice finishing touches.

Corned Beef Supper

*Nancy Wise
Little Rock, AR*

Slice any leftover corned beef for tasty sandwiches the next day.

3-lb. corned beef brisket
1 onion, thinly sliced
1 bay leaf
1 t. pepper

3-1/2 c. water
3 potatoes, peeled and cubed
4 carrots, peeled and sliced
1 cabbage, cut in wedges

Arrange brisket, onion, bay leaf and pepper in a microwave-safe 3-quart casserole dish. Add water; cover and microwave on high heat for 30 minutes. Rotate 1/4 turn; microwave on high an additional 30 minutes. Turn brisket over; add potatoes and carrots. Cover and microwave on high 10 minutes; rotate 1/4 turn and heat an additional 5 to 10 minutes until vegetables are crisp-tender. Add cabbage and mix well. Cover and microwave on high 12 to 15 minutes, until cabbage is tender. Let stand 15 minutes; test brisket for doneness. If needed, cover and microwave on high for 5 to 10 minutes longer until brisket is tender. Discard bay leaf before serving. Serves 6.

Treat yourself at home with simple soothing touches in the bathroom. Green plants, baskets of mini soaps & shampoos and big fluffy towels will create a cozy retreat for you and your family.

Meatloaf Honolulu

*Karen Stoner
Delaware, OH*

This recipe is special to us...we lived in Hawaii for 2 wonderful years.

2 lbs. ground beef	1/2 t. salt
1 c. soft bread crumbs	1/2 t. ground ginger
2 eggs, beaten	1/4 t. garlic powder
1/2 c. onion, minced	1/4 t. pepper
3 T. soy sauce, divided	1 T. all-purpose flour
2 T. brown sugar, packed and divided	1/8 t. dry mustard

Combine ground beef, bread crumbs, eggs, onion, 2 tablespoons soy sauce, one tablespoon brown sugar, salt, ginger, garlic powder and pepper. Spoon into a 6-cup microwave-safe ring mold. Microwave on high, uncovered, for 10 to 13 minutes, rotating 1/4 turn every 4 minutes, until meat begins to pull away from edges of mold. Remove from microwave and let stand, uncovered, for 5 minutes. Carefully pour drippings into a 2-cup glass measuring cup. Blend in remaining soy sauce, remaining brown sugar, flour and mustard. Add water, if necessary, to make 1/2 cup of liquid. Microwave drippings mixture for one to 3 minutes until heated through; pour over meatloaf. Microwave meatloaf, uncovered, 2 to 3 minutes. Serves 4 to 6.

Road maps make fun placemats...family members can share memories of trips they've taken or daydream about places they'd like to go. Simply cut maps to placemat size and seal in self-adhesive clear plastic.

Mexican Manicotti

Marsha Frary
Monmouth, IL

*We hope your family enjoys this recipe as much as ours does!
We usually double it...our teenage daughter can eat half of
one batch all by herself.*

1/2 lb. ground beef
1 c. refried beans
1/2 t. ground cumin
8 manicotti shells, uncooked
1 c. picante sauce
1 c. water

1/2 c. shredded Monterey Jack
 cheese
Garnish: additional picante
 sauce, sour cream, chopped
 tomato, lettuce, green onion,
 sliced black olives

Combine ground beef, beans and cumin; mix well. Fill uncooked
manicotti shells with mixture; arrange in a 10"x6" glass baking dish.
Combine picante sauce and water; pour over shells. Cover dish with
vented plastic wrap and microwave on high for 10 minutes. Using
tongs, turn shells over and rearrange them from center to outer edge
of dish. Cover again; microwave on medium at 50% power for 18 to
20 minutes, rotating dish after 10 minutes. Sprinkle with cheese;
uncover and let stand 5 minutes. Garnish as desired with sour cream,
picante sauce, tomato, lettuce, olives and onion. Makes 4 servings.

Plant scented flowers
like lilacs near your
doors and windows. The
sweet fragrance will waft
in on warm spring and
summer nights.

Mom's Best Chicken & Rice

Kay Marone
Des Moines, IA

Some sliced mushrooms make a tasty addition.

10-3/4 oz. can cream of
   mushroom soup
1-1/4 c. water
1-1/4 c. long-cooking rice,
   uncooked
1 onion, thinly sliced
1 green pepper, sliced

1 t. salt
2 to 3 lbs. boneless, skinless
   chicken breast
2 T. butter, melted
2 green onions, chopped
paprika to taste

Blend soup, water, rice, onion, green pepper and salt in a 3-quart microwave-safe casserole. Arrange chicken over mixture with large ends around edges and small in the center. Brush chicken with butter; sprinkle with green onions and paprika to taste. Cover and microwave on high for 30 to 35 minutes, rotating 1/4 turn halfway through. Let rest, covered, 10 minutes or until chicken juices run clear and rice is tender. Serves 4 to 6.

Fill empty glass jars with several inches of colored aquarium sand, Epsom salt or even craft beads, then drop a votive candle into each. Group them together for a warm glow on your dinner table.

Microwave Magic

Ham & Broccoli Baked Potatoes

Linda Behling
Cecil, PA

A quick, filling meal...easy to double and serve 4.

2 baking potatoes
1/2 c. cooked ham, chopped
1/2 c. broccoli, cooked and
    chopped

2 slices American cheese
2 t. green onion, chopped

Pierce potatoes with a fork; microwave for 6 to 8 minutes on high until tender. Cut lengthwise and crosswise; squeeze open. Top each potato with 1/4 cup each of ham and broccoli. Top each with American cheese. Microwave an additional minute or until cheese is melted; top with green onion. Serves 2.

Microwaved foods will continue to cook for several minutes after being removed from the microwave. Let your dinner stand for just a few minutes...this extra time lets the food finish cooking.

Tuna Casserole

Anita Myers
Williamsport, MD

Here's an easy way to make Grandma's favorite casserole while still keeping the kitchen cool!

12-oz. pkg. egg noodles, cooked and divided
10-3/4 oz. can cream of mushroom soup, divided
15-oz. can peas, drained and divided
6-oz. can tuna, drained and divided

salt and pepper to taste
6 slices American cheese, divided
1 c. milk
1-1/2 c. potato chips, crushed

Place half the cooked noodles in a 2-quart microwave-safe casserole. Spread half the soup over noodles, followed by half the peas and half the tuna. Add salt and pepper to taste; lay 3 slices cheese over tuna. Repeat layering with remaining ingredients. Pour milk over all; top with potato chips. Microwave on high for 12 to 15 minutes. Makes 3 to 4 servings.

An antique flat-top trunk makes a terrific coffee table with a bonus of storage space inside.

Microwave Dinner Math

Make a savory dinner in the microwave...a great way to use leftovers!

Meat		Veggies		Starch		Sauce		Add-Ins		Your Dinner
1 lb.	+	1 c. fresh, or 2 to 3 c. canned	+	2 to 3 c. cooked	+	2 cans or 2 c.	+	to taste	=	
ground beef, browned and drained	+	black olives, sliced	+	rotini pasta	+	pasta sauce	+	shredded mozzarella cheese	=	Cheesy Rotini & Beef
boneless pork, cooked and cut in strips	+	green peppers and onions, sliced	+	rice	+	teriyaki sauce (add to taste)	+	chow mein noodles	=	Teriyaki Pepper Pork
boneless, skinless chicken breasts, cooked and cubed	+	mushrooms, sliced	+	thin spaghetti	+	cream of mushroom soup	+	grated Parmesan cheese	=	Chicken Spaghetti
salmon fillets, uncooked	+	asparagus spears	+	rice	+	cream of celery soup	+	butter, dill weed, lemon juice	=	Creamy Salmon & Asparagus
3 6-1/2 oz. cans chopped clams	+	onion and celery, finely chopped	+	potatoes, diced	+	New England Clam Chowder and 2 c. milk	+	bacon bits, oyster crackers	=	Clam Chowder in a Flash

Combine all ingredients except add-ins in a microwave-safe dish. Cover with plastic; vent. Cook on high setting for 5 to 10 minutes, until heated through. Let stand several minutes; sprinkle with add-ins. Serves 4.

Use this handy formula to stir up quick meals with what you have on hand. Just copy, cut and hang on the fridge or inside a cabinet door for easy reference!

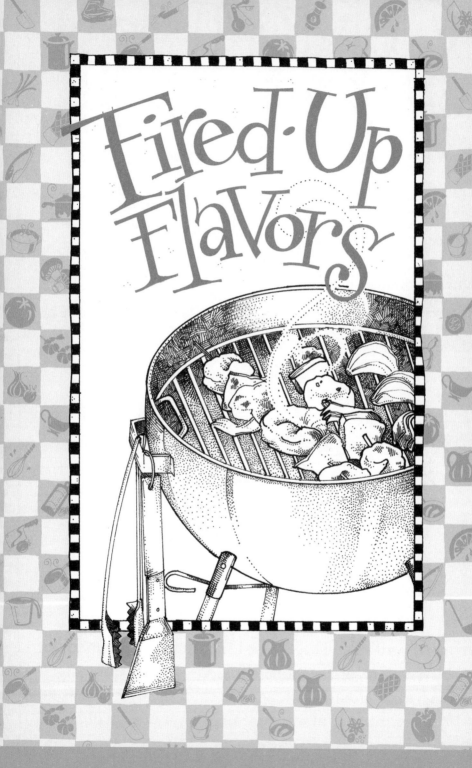

Fired·Up Flavors

GRILLING & CAMPFIRE FAVORITES

King-of-the-Road Dinner

Donna Jones
Rockport, IN

Use whatever veggies and seasoning your family likes!

4 carrots, peeled and sliced
6 potatoes, peeled and sliced
1 onion, sliced
1/2 head cabbage, sliced

10-3/4 oz. can cream of
  mushroom soup
1 to 2 lbs. Kielbasa, cut into
  bite-size slices

Arrange vegetables in an aluminum foil grilling pouch sprayed with non-stick vegetable spray. Spoon soup over vegetables; top with Kielbasa. Seal pouch tightly; set in a shallow baking pan and place on heated grill. Grill for 30 minutes; turn pouch over and grill for an additional 30 minutes. Serves 4.

For great grilling packages, use heavy-duty aluminum foil or 2 layers of regular aluminum foil. Use a piece that's large enough to go around the food and fold it tightly to seal in the juices. Be careful when opening...hot steam will be sealed in too!

Marinated Flank Steak

Shelly Biggs
Topeka, KS

A savory steak, full of flavor.

1-1/2 lbs. beef flank steak
1/2 c. soy sauce
1/4 c. red wine or beef broth
2 T. Worcestershire sauce
2 T. oil
juice of one lime

1/2 bunch green onions,
  chopped
1 clove garlic, minced
1 t. dill weed
1 t. celery seed

Place steak in a large plastic zipping bag; set aside. Combine remaining ingredients; sprinkle over steak. Seal bag and refrigerate overnight. Grill over hot coals to preferred doneness (5 to 6 minutes per side for medium-rare). Remove from grill; let steak rest for 10 minutes before slicing on the diagonal. Makes 4 servings.

Grilled Herb Potatoes

Amber Sterns
Lincoln, NE

My family loves these scrumptious potatoes!

4 potatoes
1/4 c. fresh chives, chopped and
  divided
1 c. Italian salad dressing

1 onion, sliced
4 sprigs fresh sage
salt and pepper to taste

Cut each potato into 6 wedges. Lay 3 wedges together on a double square of aluminum foil; sprinkle with one tablespoon chives and 2 tablespoons salad dressing. Place an onion slice and a sprig of sage on remaining 3 wedges. Fit potato back together and sprinkle with an additional 2 to 3 tablespoons salad dressing. Wrap tightly. Grill, covered, over medium heat for about one hour, or until potatoes are tender. Discard sage; add salt and pepper to taste. Serves 4.

· Fired-Up Flavors ·

Grilled Greek Chicken

Lena Castillo-Burnett
Los Lunas, NM

This is just a little different from the usual grilled chicken.

4 to 5 lbs. chicken
1 c. water
1/4 c. olive oil

5 lemons, divided
2 T. dried oregano
salt and pepper to taste

Place chicken pieces in a large bowl; set aside. Combine water, oil, juice of one lemon and oregano; sprinkle over chicken. Halve remaining lemons; squeeze over chicken. Cover bowl with a damp cloth and refrigerate overnight. Preheat grill to medium-low; brush with oil to prevent sticking. Arrange chicken on grill; turn every 10 minutes, basting occasionally with extra marinade. Grill for about 40 minutes, until juices run clear when pierced. Add salt and pepper to taste. Serves 4 to 6.

A clean grill makes the tastiest foods. No wire brush handy?
Simply use balls of crumpled aluminum foil as handy
scouring pads to clean the racks of your grill.

Grilled Chicken & Veggies

Deb Powers
Ankeny, IA

Make as many packages as you have guests...good served over rice.

1 boneless, skinless chicken
    breast
1/2 c. red pepper, sliced
1 carrot, peeled and sliced

1 c. broccoli flowerets
1/2 c. onion, sliced
salt and pepper to taste

Arrange chicken and vegetables on a large sheet of aluminum foil;
add salt and pepper to taste. Close aluminum foil tightly; place packet
on hot grill for 15 to 25 minutes, turning frequently, until chicken
juices run clear when pierced. Serves one.

Let the kids help prepare foil-wrapped dinners for the
family...they can mix & match their favorite veggies, meats
and flavors for your next backyard cookout.

Grilled Sausage & Veggies

Vickie

Tuck in some whole cloves of garlic or fresh herbs for extra flavor.

1-1/2 lbs. green beans, trimmed
1 lb. redskin potatoes, quartered
1 to 2 sweet onions, sliced
1-1/2 lbs. smoked sausage, cut
   in 1-inch pieces

1 t. salt
1 t. pepper
1 T. butter, sliced
1/2 c. water

Arrange beans, potatoes and onions on a large sheet of aluminum foil; top with sausage. Add salt and pepper; dot with butter. Bring up aluminum foil around ingredients; sprinkle with water and close tightly. Place packet on a hot grill; cook for 30 to 45 minutes, turning once, until sausage is browned and vegetables are tender. Serves 4.

Make grilled bread to go with dinner! Slice a loaf
of French bread nearly through. Spread slices with a mixture
of 3/4 cup shredded cheese, 1/2 cup butter, 1/4 cup
chopped fresh parsley, 1 teaspoon paprika and 3 to 4 cloves of
minced garlic. Wrap up in aluminum foil and heat on a closed
grill for about 15 minutes, turning once. Tasty!

Chuck Wagon Chops

Diana Chaney
Olathe, KS

Substitute sweet potatoes for a different taste ...use your favorite spicy flavor of barbecue sauce too!

6 bone-in pork chops
salt and pepper to taste
1 T. all-purpose flour
1/2 c. barbecue sauce

1 onion, thinly sliced
4 potatoes, peeled and cubed
1 T. oil
2 t. chili powder

Arrange pork chops without overlapping on a large sheet of aluminum foil. Add salt and pepper to taste. Stir flour into barbecue sauce; spoon over pork chops. Arrange onion slices over top. Toss together potatoes, oil and chili powder; arrange in an even layer over onion slices. Seal foil package tightly. Place on grill; cover and cook over medium-high heat for 25 to 30 minutes. Makes 4 to 6 servings.

Slip some halved, pitted ripe peaches onto the grill alongside your meat. The peaches will be hot & juicy in just a few minutes...a sweet, tasty accompaniment to grilled pork or chicken.

Scout Camp Stew

John Alexander
New Britain, CT

Fun for kids to eat right out of the foil...no dishes to wash!

1 lb. stew beef, cubed
4 potatoes, peeled and cubed
8 carrots, peeled and sliced
4 onions, chopped

4 cloves garlic, minced
salt and pepper to taste
4 T. water
4 T. butter, sliced

Divide beef and vegetables among 4 large sheets of aluminum foil. Sprinkle with garlic, salt, pepper and one tablespoon water each; dot each with one tablespoon butter. Bring together edges of aluminum foil and seal tightly. Place on a heated grill or bury in campfire coals until meat is tender, about one hour. Makes 4 servings.

Plant a garden house as a special summertime hideaway for the kids. Stand up 5 long poles teepee-style and tie together at the top. Around them, plant fast-climbing scarlet runner beans. Soon the children and their playmates will enjoy a cool, shady hiding place for playtime and make-believe.

142

Campfire Brats & Veggies

Jim Pindell
Hilliard, OH

This is so good, you won't believe how easy it is!

6 bratwurst
salt and pepper to taste
2 12-oz. cans beer

6 potatoes, cubed
4 c. broccoli flowerets
4 c. cauliflower flowerets

Sprinkle bratwurst with salt and pepper; place in a large piece of aluminum foil folded in half to make a bag. Pour beer into bag and fold closed; place in campfire close to coals. Sprinkle vegetables with salt and pepper; wrap in a separate piece of aluminum foil and place in campfire beside bratwurst. Heat slowly for 2 hours or until bratwurst have absorbed beer and vegetables are tender. Serves 6.

Campfire Onions

Jason Keller
Carrollton, GA

A tasty go-with for grilled meat.

4 sweet onions, peeled and
    quartered
4 T. butter, sliced

4 cloves garlic
salt to taste

Place each onion on a double square of aluminum foil. Place one tablespoon butter and one clove garlic in the center of each; wrap tightly. Place onions on medium-hot grill or into hot campfire coals; cook for 30 to 40 minutes or until tender. Add salt to taste. Serves 4.

Brunswick Stew

Sue Hogarth
Lancaster, CA

When I was young, every November my dad's city friends came for the first day of deer hunting season. They were never successful and came back very hungry! My mom always made big batches of this hearty stew for them outdoors in a Dutch oven on a tripod over an open fire. What a wonderful day of friendship and blessings!

2 slices bacon
1 c. onion, chopped
3 lbs. chicken
2 10-3/4 oz. cans chicken broth
2-1/4 c. water, divided
1/3 c. celery, chopped
2 t. salt
16-oz. can stewed tomatoes

2 c. potatoes, peeled and diced
10-oz. pkg. frozen okra, thawed
10-oz. pkg. frozen baby lima
   beans, thawed
12-oz. can corn, drained
1 T. Worcestershire sauce
3 T. all-purpose flour

Sauté together bacon and onion in a 4-quart Dutch oven until onion is golden, about 5 minutes. Remove bacon mixture from Dutch oven; set aside. Place chicken, broth, 2 cups water, celery, salt and bacon mixture in Dutch oven. Bring to a boil; reduce heat and simmer, covered, 45 minutes or just until chicken is tender. Skim fat. Remove bones from chicken; discard and return meat to pot. Add tomatoes, potatoes, okra and lima beans. Bring to a boil; reduce heat and simmer, covered, 15 minutes or until potatoes are tender. Add corn and Worcestershire sauce; heat to boiling. Mix flour with remaining water in a small bowl; stir into broth. Heat and stir until thickened. Makes 6 servings.

Need to remove excess fat
from homemade soup?
Simply dip a lettuce leaf
into the soup.

Woodland Wild Rice

Dale-Harriet Rogovich
Madison, WI

My husband and I have taken this dish camping many times. We love it! Sometimes we add pecans or dried cranberries for variety.

2 lbs. ground country-style
    sausage
1 to 2 sweet onions, sliced
16-oz. pkg. sliced mushrooms

16-oz. pkg. wild rice, uncooked
2 10-3/4 oz. cans cream of
    mushroom soup

Sauté together sausage and onions in a large Dutch oven until browned. Add mushrooms and sauté for 4 to 5 additional minutes. Drain and remove from Dutch oven; set aside. Cook wild rice in Dutch oven according to package directions until nearly tender, about 45 minutes. Combine rice with sausage mixture; fold in soup and mix well. Heat through. Makes 4 to 8 servings.

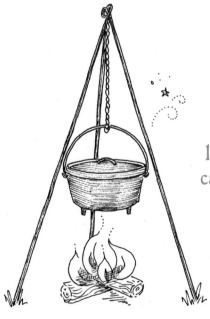

Remember to tote along some blankets or folding stools when you go camping...there's nothing like sitting around a glowing campfire stargazing, swapping stories and just savoring time together with friends & family!

Mom's Vegetable Soup

Barbara Cissell
Louisville, KY

During the Depression, my mother-in-law fed 14 kids with this soup, using whatever ingredients she had on hand. It's still wonderful and tastes even better the second day.

6 c. water
7 potatoes, peeled and chopped
1/2 head cabbage, shredded
1 to 2 onions, chopped
16-oz. can mixed vegetables
16-oz. can peas, drained

2 8-oz. cans tomato sauce
1-1/2 c. elbow macaroni,
    uncooked
1/2 c. bacon drippings
2 t. salt
1 t. pepper

Place water in a 5-quart stockpot. Add potatoes, cabbage and onions; bring to a rolling boil. Reduce heat, cover and simmer for 10 minutes or until potatoes are tender. Stir in remaining ingredients; add more water as needed to fill pot. Return to a rolling boil; simmer, covered, for 20 minutes or until soup is thickened and macaroni is tender. Add additional salt and pepper to taste. Makes 12 to 14 servings.

Camp cooking is extra-easy when you chop or shred veggies and cheese at home, then pack in plastic zipping bags. Pack potatoes and apples whole, though, so they won't turn dark.

Moutinho Family Stew

Christine Moutinho Bentley
Palm Coast, FL

This soup is definitely a meal in itself.

1/2 t. garlic, minced
1/2 c. onion, finely chopped
2 T. oil
1 lb. stew beef, cubed
1/2 t. Italian seasoning
1/8 t. garlic powder

1/8 t. pepper
1/8 t. dried basil
2 8-oz. cans tomato sauce
12-oz. pkg. shell macaroni,
    uncooked

Sauté garlic and onion in oil in a stockpot. Add beef; heat until brown, about 20 minutes. Sprinkle meat with seasonings; add tomato sauce. Add water to cover meat; lower heat and simmer for about 2 hours. Add enough additional water to cook macaroni; heat to boiling and stir in macaroni. Simmer about 10 minutes, until macaroni is tender. Serves 6.

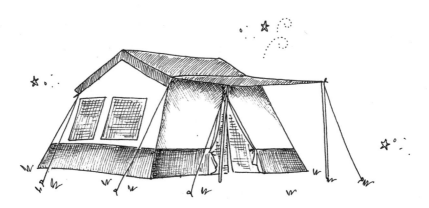

Have a backyard campout! Set up the tent and bring out camp chairs, sleeping bags and a portable grill. When the sun goes down, you can count fireflies, watch for shooting stars and make s'mores together. What a great occasion for family time!

Santa Fe Cheese Soup

Andrea Pocreva
San Antonio, TX

Good and cheesy!

1 lb. ground beef
1 onion, chopped
15-oz. can ranch-style beans,
  drained

14-1/2 oz. can diced tomatoes
15-1/4 oz. can corn, drained
1 lb. pasteurized processed
  cheese spread, cubed

Brown together ground beef and onion in a stockpot; drain. Stir in remaining ingredients. Simmer about 15 to 20 minutes, or until cheese is melted. Serves 8.

Bring along trail mix for those times when a campfire dinner takes a little longer than expected. Toss together peanuts, raisins, sunflower kernels and fish-shaped crackers and fill some little zipping bags...a lifesaver for growling tummies!

Fiesta Beef Soup

Tina Lewis
Seminole, OK

This hearty soup is a great meal for cold days. Garnish with tortilla chips, sour cream and shredded cheese.

1 lb. ground beef
15-oz. can ranch-style beans, drained
14-1/2 oz. can tomatoes with chiles

14-1/2 oz. can stewed tomatoes
11-oz. can corn with diced peppers, drained
1-1/4 oz. pkg. taco seasoning mix

Brown ground beef in a stockpot; drain. Stir in remaining ingredients; lower heat and simmer for 15 to 20 minutes until heated through. Serves 6 to 8.

Declare a Picnic Night at home! Just toss a checkered tablecloth on the dinner table and set out paper plates and disposable plastic utensils. Relax and enjoy dinner...no dishes to wash!

Baked Bean Stew

Sandy Westendorp
Grand Rapids, MI

This tasty stew is extra-easy to pack for camping out. Just substitute 2 to 3 cans of chicken for the fresh chicken.

1 c. onion, chopped
1 c. green pepper, chopped
1 T. oil
3/4 lb. boneless, skinless
    chicken breasts, chopped
14-1/2 oz. can diced tomatoes
    with chili seasoning

2 15-oz. cans pork & beans
15-oz. can garbanzo beans,
    drained and rinsed
3/4 t. dried sage
1/2 t. ground cumin
salt and pepper to taste

In a large saucepan, sauté onion and green pepper in oil until tender. Add chicken and cook over medium heat until golden. Add tomatoes, beans and herbs to saucepan; heat to boiling. Reduce heat and simmer, uncovered, for 8 to 10 minutes. Add salt and pepper to taste. Serves 8.

Try something new when making s'mores...substitute chocolate-covered peppermint patties for plain chocolate bars for a fresh new taste!

Campers' Stew

Marty Laform
San Jose, CA

We've made this with our Girl Scout troop for years. It smells delicious in the kitchen or over an open fire! It's great with cornbread.

1 lb. ground beef
1 onion, chopped
4 potatoes, peeled and cubed
5 carrots, peeled and sliced

1 green pepper, chopped
29-oz. can tomato sauce
3-1/2 c. water
salt and pepper to taste

Sauté ground beef and onion together in a 5-quart stockpot; drain. Stir in remaining ingredients; simmer for 30 to 45 minutes, until vegetables are tender. Serves 4.

Fill empty plastic soda bottles with water, then freeze. Packed in your camp cooler, they'll keep your food fresh, and as they melt, you'll have fresh icy water handy to quench your thirst.

Pioneer Stew

Joy Young
Oklahoma City, OK

A pot full of hot stew bubbling over the campfire...there's nothing better on a cool fall day!

1-1/2 lbs. ground beef
1 onion, chopped
1 green pepper, chopped
16-oz. can pinto beans, drained
   and rinsed
14-1/2 oz. can diced tomatoes

15-1/2 oz. can kidney beans,
   drained and rinsed
15-1/4 oz. can corn, drained
chili powder to taste
1 c. shredded Cheddar cheese

Brown ground beef, onion and green pepper together in a large stockpot; drain. Add all remaining ingredients except shredded cheese. Simmer together until heated through and flavors are blended, 30 to 40 minutes. Stir in cheese until melted. Serves 4 to 6.

The kids will love making biscuits on a stick! Mix up some dough with biscuit baking mix. Then take a fist-sized piece of dough, roll between hands into long ropes and wind around a long green stick. Hold over hot coals until golden. Butter well and sprinkle with cinnamon-sugar if you like!

Hearty Sausage Stew

Darrell Lawry
Kissimmee, FL

Wonderful homemade flavor...tastes even better the next day.

1 lb. Polish sausage, thickly
    sliced
2 16-oz. cans kidney beans,
    drained and rinsed
29-oz. can stewed tomatoes
1 to 2 potatoes, diced

1 onion, chopped
1/2 green pepper, chopped
4 c. water
1 clove garlic, minced
1 bay leaf
salt and pepper to taste

In a large saucepan, sauté sausage until browned; drain. Add
remaining ingredients. Simmer for 45 minutes to one hour, or until
heated through. Discard bay leaf. Serves 4 to 6.

Nature knows no difference between weeds and flowers.
-Mason Cooley

Chicken & Barley Stew

Marcy Dotson
Prospect, CT

This is a family favorite for harvest time in the fall.

1/4 c. butter
2 T. all-purpose flour
2-1/2 c. water
3 cubes chicken bouillon
2 boneless, skinless chicken
    breasts, cubed
1/2 c. pearled barley
2 carrots, peeled and sliced
2 stalks celery, sliced

2 T. dried thyme
20 cherry tomatoes
4-oz. can whole mushrooms,
    drained
1 bunch green onions, sliced
1/8 t. browning and seasoning
    sauce
salt and pepper to taste

Melt butter over low heat in a large stockpot; stir in flour. Gradually stir in water and bouillon cubes, stirring constantly. Add chicken, barley, carrots, celery and thyme. Simmer over medium heat for 30 minutes, stirring frequently. Add remaining ingredients; simmer for 2 additional hours, stirring occasionally. Crush softened tomatoes with a spoon before serving. Serves 6 to 8.

Try packing pita bread, flatbread or tortillas for camping, instead of regular loaf bread. They won't crush when packed...tasty warmed up on a griddle over the fire too.

Hearty Cabbage Stew

Christine Youngblood
Weatherford, TX

*Chock-full of veggies, a steaming cup of this soup is just the thing
to greet you after a long hike in brisk weather.*

1 lb. ground beef
1 onion, chopped
1 T. chili powder
1 head cabbage, chopped
2 stalks celery, chopped
1 green pepper, chopped
15-1/4 oz. can corn, drained
14-1/2 oz. can tomatoes with
   chiles

14-1/2 oz. can diced tomatoes
14-1/2 oz. can sliced carrots,
   drained
15-oz. can ranch-style beans,
   drained
8-oz. can tomato sauce
1 t. garlic salt
1 t. salt
1 t. pepper

Sauté together ground beef, onion and chili powder in a stockpot;
drain. Add remaining ingredients; reduce heat and simmer for
45 minutes to one hour. Makes 4 to 6 servings.

Stencil a favorite saying or a flower pattern on a wooden
bench. When dry, the bench can hold a row of potted flowers
or rest in a shady spot as a garden getaway for you.

Camp Chowder

Kathy Grashoff
Fort Wayne, IN

A hearty seafood soup that's ready in just a few minutes.

4 slices bacon
1/4 c. onion, chopped
2 T. green pepper, chopped
1 clove garlic, minced
10-3/4 oz. can cream of potato
   soup

2 c. milk
6-oz. can tuna, drained
6-1/2 oz. can chopped clams,
   drained
Garnish: paprika

Sauté bacon in a large saucepan until crisp. Remove from pan and set aside; drain most of drippings. Add onion, green pepper and garlic to pan; heat for 4 to 5 minutes until tender. Add soup and milk; simmer for several minutes. Add tuna, clams and reserved bacon; heat until warmed through. Sprinkle with paprika. Serves 4 to 6.

Send the kids to hunt for pine cones when you're camping...they're a nice year-round accent in a basket on the hearth and a great craft material when the holidays approach.

Salmon & Potato Chowder

John Kinnison
Ottawa, IL

Whole peppercorns add extra flavor, but if you prefer, substitute
1/4 teaspoon of coarsely ground pepper.

14-3/4 oz. can pink salmon
3 potatoes, peeled and diced
1-3/4 c. water
1 onion, chopped
4 whole peppercorns

12-oz. can evaporated milk
1 T. fresh dill, chopped
pepper to taste
Garnish: lemon wedges

Rinse salmon for one minute in a colander under cold water; set aside.
Combine potatoes, water, onion and peppercorns in a large saucepan.
Bring to a boil; reduce heat and simmer for 20 minutes, until potatoes
are tender. Stir in milk, salmon, dill and pepper; heat through. Discard
peppercorns before serving, if desired. Garnish with lemon wedges.
Serves 6.

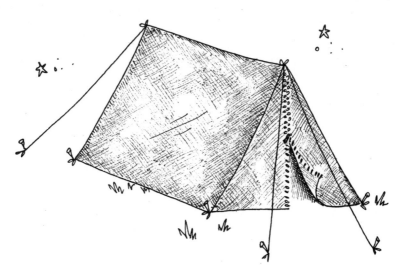

Oh, for the simple life,
For tents and starry skies!
-Israel Zangwill

"Grilling Dinner Math"

When it's too nice to stay inside...throw together a great dinner on the grill!

Meat (1 to 2 lbs. uncooked)	Veggies (1-1/2 to 2 c. fresh, one or more)	Starch (1-1/2 to 2 c.)	Sauce (to taste)	Add-Ins (to taste)	Your Dinner
ground beef patties	+ tomatoes, sliced	+ potatoes, sliced or quartered	+ barbecue sauce	+ French fried onions	= Barbecued Burgers
Kielbasa, halved	+ green beans	+ potatoes, sliced or quartered	+ beer or beef broth	+ spicy mustard	= Biergarten Dinner
boneless pork chops	+ corn on the cob, halved	+ sweet potatoes, sliced	+ butter, minced garlic	+ chives, chopped	= Down-Home Pork Chops & Corn
boneless, skinless chicken breasts	+ red and green pepper, onion, sliced	+ soft flour tortillas (spoon into after grilling)	+ salsa	+ shredded Cheddar cheese, sour cream	= Grilled Chicken Fajitas
large shrimp and/or cod fillets	+ zucchini or yellow squash, sliced	+ cooked rice (serve with after grilling)	+ butter, dill weed, lemon juice	+ paprika	= Dilled Shrimp & Squash

Divide meat among 4 lengths of heavy-duty aluminum foil. Arrange veggies over meat and top with seasoning. Crimp foil tightly to form 4 packages. Place on a heated grill for 25 to 30 minutes (meats); 15 to 20 minutes (seafood). Top with add-ins. Serves 4.

Use this handy formula to stir up quick meals with what you have on hand. Just copy, cut and hang on the fridge or inside a cabinet door for easy reference!

Cool as a Cucumber

HEARTY DINNER SALADS FROM THE FRIDGE

· Cool as a Cucumber ·

Lemon-Herb Chicken Salad

Barbara Stienstra
Goshen, NY

The lemon-herb dressing makes this chicken salad just a little different. It's especially good with croissants.

2 boneless, skinless chicken
    breasts, cooked and diced
1/4 c. mayonnaise
1/4 c. yogurt

1 T. fresh dill, chopped
2 t. lemon juice
1/2 t. lemon zest
1/4 t. salt

Place chicken in a serving bowl; set aside. Combine remaining ingredients; mix well and toss with chicken. Chill before serving. Serves 4 to 6.

Raisin-Pecan Chicken Salad

Theresa Beach
Lexington, SC

Sometimes we like to add a little pineapple juice for extra zing.

12-1/2 oz. can chicken, drained
2 stalks celery, chopped
1 c. golden raisins
1/2 c. chopped pecans
3/4 c. mayonnaise

1 c. sour cream
Optional: 1/4 c. red onion,
    minced
1 t. salt
1 t. pepper

Mix all ingredients together; chill before serving. Makes 2 to 4 servings.

Hollowed-out fruits make refreshing salad servers. Try scooping out grapefruits or pineapples...toss the fruit with honey dressing to serve on the side.

Chicken-Artichoke & Rice Salad

Charlotte Mitchell
Anchorage, AK

Sprinkle with sunflower kernels for extra crunch.

4.7-oz. pkg. chicken-flavored
   rice vermicelli mix, cooked
2 c. cooked chicken, diced
2 2-1/4 oz. jars marinated
   artichoke hearts, drained
   and 1 jar liquid reserved
1 green pepper, chopped

1 bunch green onions, chopped
8-oz. can water chestnuts,
   drained and chopped
2/3 c. mayonnaise
1/2 t. curry powder
1/8 t. salt
1/8 t. pepper

Combine rice vermicelli mix and chicken in a serving bowl; set aside.
Chop artichokes; add to mixture along with reserved liquid. Blend in
remaining ingredients; chill before serving. Makes 3 to 4 servings.

Invite friends over for a Salad Supper on a day that's too hot
to cook. Ask everyone to bring along a favorite salad. You
provide crispy bread sticks or a basket of tea muffins and a
pitcher of iced tea...relax and enjoy!

Hawaiian Chicken-Pasta Salad

Mary Patenaude
Griswold, CT

Keep the kitchen cool...pick up a rotisserie chicken from the grocery.

8-oz. pkg. penne pasta, cooked
2 c. boneless, skinless chicken
   breasts, cooked and diced
11-oz. can mandarin oranges,
   drained

8-oz. can pineapple tidbits,
   drained and juice reserved
3/4 c. celery, sliced
3/4 c. chopped walnuts
1/4 c. onion, chopped

Rinse penne with cold water; drain well. Combine all ingredients except pineapple juice and mix well. Pour dressing over the top; toss to coat. Chill before serving. Serves 8.

Dressing:

1/2 c. mayonnaise
1/3 c. sour cream

2 T. reserved pineapple juice
1/2 t. salt

Mix all ingredients together; use a whisk to blend well.

A splash of ginger ale in orange juice makes a refreshing drink to accompany a cool salad. Serve in a tall glass with lots of ice...aaah!

Chinese Chicken Salad

Joanne Zenker
Annapolis, MD

The seasoning packets from the ramen noodles aren't used in this recipe...save them for seasoning soups or casseroles.

4 c. boneless, skinless chicken
    breasts, cooked and diced
1 head cabbage, finely chopped
3 to 4 green onions, chopped
2 to 3 stalks celery, chopped

1 onion, diced
1 red pepper, diced
2 3-oz. pkgs. ramen noodles,
    crushed
Garnish: 1/2 c. sliced almonds

Place all ingredients except nuts in a serving bowl; do not use ramen noodle seasoning packets. Toss with dressing to coat. Refrigerate for 3 to 4 hours. At serving time, sprinkle with nuts. Serves 8.

Dressing:

3/4 c. olive oil
1/4 c. sesame oil
6 T. rice vinegar
1/4 c. sugar
2 t. salt

2 t. sesame seed
1 t. celery seed
1 t. pepper
Cajun seasoning to taste

Mix all ingredients together; stir well.

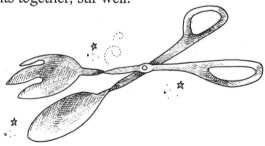

Tote creamy salads to potlucks the no-spill way...packed in a large plastic zipping bag. When you arrive, simply pour the salad into a serving bowl.

Pizza Pasta Salad

Julia List
Lincoln, NE

This salad has such a wonderful tangy flavor and it's always a hit at potlucks and cookouts. It complements any meal and there are rarely any leftovers...be sure to help yourself first!

16-oz. pkg. tri-color rotini
2 tomatoes, seeded and diced
6-oz. can black olives, drained
1 sweet onion, sliced
1/2 lb. Cheddar cheese, cubed
1/2 lb. mozzarella cheese, cubed
3-oz. pkg. sliced pepperoni
3/4 c. oil

3/4 c. grated Parmesan cheese
1/2 c. red wine vinegar
2 t. dried oregano
1 t. garlic powder
1 t. salt
1/4 t. pepper
cayenne pepper to taste

Prepare pasta according to package directions; drain and rinse with cold water. In a large serving bowl, mix pasta, vegetables, Cheddar and mozzarella cheeses and pepperoni; set aside. In a separate bowl, whisk remaining ingredients together; pour over pasta mixture. Stir; cover and refrigerate until serving. Serves 16.

Turn a tube of refrigerated biscuits into quick & easy garlic biscuits. Place biscuits in a greased 9" round baking pan. Top each with a pat of butter, then shake on garlic powder and grated Parmesan cheese to taste. Bake until golden as package directs.

Antipasto Salad

Christa Kerr
DuBois, PA

For a pretty presentation, arrange the ingredients in sections on a large platter...just sprinkle with salad dressing.

16-oz. pkg. frozen cheese-filled
   tortellini, cooked
1 lb. sliced deli ham, cut into
   1-inch squares
1/2 lb. sliced salami, quartered
1/4 lb. sliced pepperoni
1/2 lb. provolone cheese, cubed
1/2 lb. Swiss cheese, cubed

1/2 lb. mozzarella cheese, cubed
6-oz. can black olives, drained
6-oz. jar green olives, drained
2 green peppers, sliced
1 sweet onion, halved and sliced
16-oz. bottle Italian salad
   dressing

Rinse tortellini with cold water; drain well. Combine all ingredients except dressing in a large bowl. Pour dressing over the top; stir until mixed well. Chill before serving. Serves 8 to 10.

Welcome guests with a year 'round wreath. Start with a grapevine wreath, then add greenery, decorations and a homespun bow to match...bunnies and eggs for spring, mini flags and sparkly stars for summer and other items for fall and winter. Store everything in a box kept handy for greeting the next season.

Garden-Fresh Gazpacho ▶

Patsy Johnson
Salem, MO

I learned to make this when I was managing a restaurant. It can be very addictive in the summer months...almost like a salad in a glass!

6 to 8 tomatoes, chopped
1 onion, finely chopped
1 cucumber, peeled and chopped
1 green pepper, chopped
2 T. fresh parsley or cilantro, chopped
1 clove garlic, finely chopped

1 to 2 stalks celery, chopped
2 T. lemon juice
salt and pepper to taste
4 c. tomato juice
4 drops hot pepper sauce
Optional: sour cream

Combine all ingredients except sour cream, if using, in a large lidded container or gallon-size Mason jar. Refrigerate until well chilled. Dollop servings with sour cream, if desired. Serves 12 to 15.

Empty jars make handy vases when your child brings you a hand-picked bouquet. Use them, too, when you take flowers to a new mom or a shut-in friend...no need for the "vase" to be returned to you. Tie a raffia bow around the jar for a sweet touch.

Mediterranean Pasta Salad

Mary Rose Kulczak
Lambertville, MI

For variety, substitute grated Parmesan cheese for feta cheese and Italian olive oil dressing for the balsamic vinaigrette.

12-oz. pkg. bowtie pasta, cooked
12-oz. jar marinated artichoke
   hearts, drained and chopped
2-1/4 oz. can sliced black olives,
   drained
1 cucumber, chopped

1 pt. cherry tomatoes
3 T. sweet onion, chopped
8-oz. bottle balsamic vinaigrette
   salad dressing
6-oz. pkg. crumbled feta cheese

Rinse pasta with cold water; drain well. Toss together all ingredients except cheese. Refrigerate for 2 to 3 hours. Before serving, toss with cheese. Serves 8 to 10.

Happiness always looks small while you hold it
in your hands, but let it go and you learn at once
how big and precious it is.
-Maxim Gorky

Southwestern Cornbread Salad

Becky Newton
Oklahoma City, OK

A yummy mix of flavors and textures. It's easy to cut this recipe in half if you aren't feeding a crowd.

8-oz. pkg. Mexican cornbread
   mix
2 16-oz. cans pinto beans,
   drained
3 tomatoes, chopped
1/2 c. green pepper, chopped
1/2 c. green onion, chopped
16-oz. can corn, drained

2 c. shredded Cheddar cheese
1 c. mayonnaise
1 c. sour cream
1-1/2 oz. pkg. ranch salad
   dressing mix
1 lb. bacon, crisply cooked
   and crumbled

Prepare cornbread according to package directions; let cool. Crumble half the cornbread into a large bowl. Layer with one can of beans and half the tomatoes, green pepper, onion, corn and shredded cheese; set aside. Combine mayonnaise, sour cream and ranch dressing mix; spread half over shredded cheese layer. Sprinkle with half the bacon. Repeat layering as before, ending with mayonnaise mixture and bacon. Chill. Serves 12 to 14.

Set a pot of chives by the kitchen door for summer-long flavor. In spring, the purple blossoms can be added to white vinegar to give it a delightful pink tint and oniony flavor.

Panzella Bread Salad

Annmarie Heavey
Bridgewater, MA

This traditional Italian bread salad began as a thrifty way to use up day-old bread. Now we make it just because it's delicious!

4 c. Italian bread, torn into
  bite-size pieces
5 tomatoes, diced
1/2 red onion, sliced
1/2 cucumber, peeled, quartered
  and sliced

1/2 c. fresh basil, chopped
3 cloves garlic, minced
3 T. red wine vinegar
4 T. olive oil
1/2 t. salt
pepper to taste

Combine bread, vegetables, basil and garlic; toss well. Sprinkle with vinegar, oil, salt and pepper. Let stand at room temperature for 1-1/2 to 2 hours before serving so the bread can absorb the dressing. Serves 4 to 6.

Get mouths watering in anticipation with a
big ceramic serving bowl just for salad or pasta.

• Cool as a Cucumber •

Bratwurst & Potato Salad

Myron Schirer-Suter
Los Angeles, CA

Toasted, buttered dark rye bread goes well with this salad.

6 bratwurst
1/4 c. bacon drippings or oil
2 lbs. redskin potatoes,
    quartered and boiled
1 bunch green onions, thinly
    sliced

1/2 c. olive oil
3 T. white wine vinegar
2 T. German mustard
salt and pepper to taste
Optional: 1/8 t. sugar

Cook bratwurst according to package instructions; brown in bacon drippings or oil. Cut into one-inch pieces. Combine bratwurst, potatoes and green onions in a large bowl; set aside. Mix remaining ingredients together; pour over bratwurst mixture and toss to coat. Refrigerate overnight. Serves 6 to 8.

Stencil stair risers with positive words like "Hope," "Joy" and "Peace" in country colors...barn red, deep blue, mustard yellow. Even the simplest stenciled letters add a charming folky touch.

Southwestern Chicken-Potato Salad

Carol Hickman
Kingsport, TN

Sprinkle in some diced green chiles for extra color and flavor.

6 potatoes, peeled, boiled and
    cubed
1-1/2 c. boneless, skinless
    chicken breast, cooked
    and diced

15-1/2 oz. can corn, drained
1 tomato, chopped
1/4 c. mayonnaise
1/4 c. sour cream
1/4 c. salsa

Combine potatoes, chicken, corn and tomato in a serving bowl; set aside. Blend remaining ingredients; fold gently into potato mixture. Stir to coat; refrigerate for at least 30 minutes before serving. Serves 4 to 6.

Make a seed packet garden pail. Cut out flower and vegetable pictures and glue to an enameled pail, then coat the pail with a clear waterproof sealer. Place a flowering plant inside and hang on a garden fence. For winter, use Christmas card cutouts and add sprigs of holly.

Tuna Seashell Salad

Susan Brees
Lincoln, NE

I took this yummy salad to a potluck party and it won 1st place!

16-oz. pkg. shell macaroni,
  cooked
12-oz. can tuna, drained
3 eggs, hard-boiled, peeled
  and diced

4-oz. pkg. mild Cheddar cheese,
  diced
1/2 to 1 c. mayonnaise-type
  salad dressing
1/4 c. sweet pickle relish

Rinse macaroni with cold water; drain well. Combine all ingredients in a large serving bowl; chill. Serves 6 to 8.

Crabby Tuna Salad

Joan Dove
Millersville, MD

You'll be happy, not crabby, when you taste this salad!

2 c. prepared elbow macaroni
6-oz. can tuna, drained
1/4 to 1/2 c. mayonnaise

2 T. onion, chopped
2 T. celery, chopped
2 T. seafood seasoning

Rinse macaroni with cold water; drain well. Mix macaroni and tuna with enough mayonnaise to moisten; add onion, celery and seasoning. Mix well and chill. Serves 3 to 4.

Decorate a pillar candle with sparkly sand and tiny shells brought back from a seaside vacation. Simply brush craft glue on the candle, sprinkle with sand and press in shells.

Blue Crab Salad

Kathy Unruh
Fresno, CA

*Try flatbread or water crackers as a great accompaniment
to this salad.*

6 cloves garlic, minced
2 shallots, minced
1/4 c. oil
1/2 c. sour cream
2-oz. pkg. Boursin cheese,
   softened
1-1/2 t. green hot pepper sauce

1/4 t. Worcestershire sauce
1 T. fresh cilantro, chopped
2 T. fresh chives, chopped
juice of 2 limes
1 t. salt
cayenne pepper to taste
1 lb. crabmeat

Sauté garlic and shallots in oil just until translucent; remove from heat. In a medium bowl, blend sour cream and Boursin cheese; stir in hot pepper sauce, Worcestershire sauce, cilantro and chives. Sprinkle in lime juice and cayenne pepper. Mix in garlic mixture and crabmeat, being careful not to break up the crabmeat too fine. Serves 6 to 8.

An ice bowl makes a cool server for seafood salad. Center a
small plastic bowl inside a larger one, using masking tape to
hold in place. Arrange citrus slices and sprigs of mint
between the bowls, fill with water and freeze until solid.
Gently remove both plastic bowls and fill with salad.

Shrimp Deluxe Summer Salad

Amanda Shelata
Oakley, CA

Shrimply delicious!

2 lbs. frozen salad shrimp, thawed
2 heads lettuce, shredded
1-1/2 c. celery, chopped
1-1/2 c. green onion, chopped

1 c. fresh parsley, chopped
10-oz. pkg. frozen petite green peas, thawed
2 c. mayonnaise
1-1/2 c. chow mein noodles

Combine all ingredients except chow mein noodles in a serving bowl; toss lightly. Chill. Just before serving, sprinkle with noodles. Serves 6 to 8.

Serve a tasty dill butter with crisp bread sticks. Soften 1/2 cup butter, then blend in 2 teaspoons dill weed, 2 teaspoons fresh chives and 1 teaspoon lemon juice. Great with seafood!

Shrimp Pasta Salad

Debra Donaldson
Florala, AL

This cool, refreshing salad is scrumptious! I serve it with sliced cheese, crackers, fresh fruit and sweet tea.

1-1/2 c. prepared elbow
   macaroni
1 lb. frozen salad shrimp,
   thawed
1 c. frozen green peas, thawed
1 red pepper, sliced

1 c. mayonnaise
2 eggs, hard-boiled, peeled
   and diced
2 T. onion, minced
seasoned salt and pepper to
   taste

Rinse macaroni in cold water. Drain macaroni, shrimp and peas well; combine in a large bowl and set aside. Chop red pepper in a blender. Add mayonnaise and blend until the mayonnaise turns pink; set aside. Add eggs and onion to shrimp mixture; stir in mayonnaise mixture. Sprinkle with seasoned salt and pepper. Serves 4.

Bread, Crab & Shrimp Salad

Debbie Meyer
Sacramento, CA

Use all shrimp or all crab if you prefer.

1 loaf French bread, crusts
   trimmed
4 to 5 eggs, hard-boiled, peeled
   and diced
1 onion, diced
1-1/2 lbs. frozen salad shrimp,
   thawed

1-1/2 lbs. crabmeat, cooked
1 c. celery, diced
3 c. mayonnaise-type salad
   dressing
1 t. seasoned salt flavor
   enhancer
Garnish: paprika

Cube bread; combine with eggs and onion in a bowl. Cover and refrigerate overnight. Add remaining ingredients except paprika. Cover and refrigerate several hours. Sprinkle with paprika. Serves 4 to 6.

Goalpost Apple Slaw ▶️

Mary Romack
Ann Arbor, MI

So crisp, cool and crunchy...a tailgating favorite!

2-1/4 c. red apples, cored
   and cubed
2-1/4 c. green apples, cored
   and cubed
1 c. coleslaw mix
1/3 c. sweetened dried
   cranberries
1/3 c. chopped walnuts

1 c. sour cream
3 T. lemon juice
1 to 2 T. vinegar
1 T. sugar
1 T. poppy seed
3/4 t. salt
1/8 t. pepper

Lightly toss ingredients in a large bowl until well mixed. Chill for
at least one hour before serving. Serves 6 to 8.

Greek Orzo Salad

Leslie Stimel
Westerville, OH

This salad is my own creation...feel free to add or subtract any
of these ingredients to suit your own taste!

1/3 c. roasted red peppers, diced
1/4 c. kalamata olives, diced
1 tomato, diced

2 c. prepared orzo pasta
1/2 c. crumbled feta cheese
balsamic vinegar to taste

Combine peppers, olives and tomato in a medium bowl; set aside.
Rinse orzo with cold water; drain well. Add orzo and feta cheese to
pepper mixture; mix well. Drizzle with vinegar; stir again. Serve warm
or chilled. Serves 4.

Spinach Salad

Jackie Crough
Salina, KS

Crisply cooked bacon bits make a tasty addition.

2 10-oz. pkgs. frozen chopped
   spinach, thawed and drained
1/2 c. onion, chopped
1/2 c. celery, chopped
3 eggs, hard-boiled, peeled
   and chopped

1 c. shredded Cheddar cheese
1-1/4 c. mayonnaise
2 t. prepared horseradish
1-1/2 t. vinegar
1/2 t. hot pepper sauce
1/2 t. salt

Combine spinach, onion, celery, eggs and cheese; mix well. Set aside. Mix remaining ingredients together; toss with spinach mixture. Cover; chill. Serves 6 to 8.

Microwave raw onions on high in a covered container for one to 2 minutes before using. They'll be easier to peel and will also lose some of the "hot" taste...helpful to know if you're serving them uncooked in salads or on hamburgers and sandwiches.

My Favorite Broccoli Salad

Darlene Hartzler
Marshallville, OH

This salad is so yummy, crunchy and good...mmm!

1 bunch broccoli, chopped
1 head cauliflower, chopped
1 c. tomato, chopped
1/3 c. onion, chopped
1 lb. bacon, crisply cooked and
   crumbled

2 eggs, hard-boiled, peeled
   and sliced
1 c. mayonnaise
1/3 c. sugar
2 T. vinegar

Combine broccoli, cauliflower, tomato, onion, bacon and eggs in a large bowl; chill. In a small bowl, mix mayonnaise, sugar and vinegar until smooth; toss with broccoli mixture just before serving. Makes 8 to 10 servings.

Dress up glasses of lemonade or iced tea by dipping the rims into lemon juice, then into sparkling sugar.

Sandra's Pomegranate Salad ▶

Sandra Smith
Lancaster, CA

Here in California, people have pomegranate trees in their yards, and we had three such trees at our old house. I also make pomegranate jelly and a pomegranate cordial, but this salad is a favorite.

2 bunches arugula, torn
2 ripe pears, halved, cored and
    cut into wedges
2 T. lime juice
2 T. olive oil
1/2 t. Dijon mustard
salt and pepper to taste

seeds of 1 pomegranate
Optional: 1/2 c. crumbled feta
    cheese, 1/3 c. toasted
    chopped pecans
Garnish: Boston or Bibb lettuce
    leaves

Place arugula and pears in a large salad bowl; set aside. In a small bowl, whisk together lime juice, olive oil and mustard. Toss arugula and pears with just enough lime juice mixture to coat; season with salt and pepper. Sprinkle salad with pomegranate seeds; add cheese and pecans, if using. Line 6 salad plates with lettuce leaves; place a serving of salad in the center of each. Serves 6.

Redecorating? Cover hatboxes with matching wallpaper...
handy storage with a coordinated look.

Teriyaki Beef Salad

Carol Lytle
Columbus, OH

Chow mein noodles make a crispy topping for this salad.

3 c. deli roast beef, cut in
    thin strips
2 tomatoes, cut in wedges
1 green pepper, cut in strips
1 c. sliced mushrooms
1 c. celery, sliced

1/2 c. green onion, thinly sliced
1/2 c. teriyaki sauce
1/3 c. oil
1/4 c. vinegar
1/2 t. ginger
4 c. mixed salad greens

Combine beef, tomatoes, green pepper, mushrooms, celery and green onion in a large plastic zipping bag; set aside. Stir together remaining ingredients except salad greens in a small bowl; pour over beef mixture in bag. Toss well and refrigerate for 3 to 4 hours. At serving time, toss beef mixture again; drain excess dressing. Divide greens among 4 salad plates and top with beef mixture. Makes 4 servings.

A small house will hold as much happiness as a big one.
-Unknown

BBQ Beef & Wagon Wheels Salad

Samantha Starks
Madison, WI

A hearty dinner salad for cowboy-size appetites.

2 c. prepared wagon wheel pasta
1 c. deli roast beef, cut in thin strips
3/4 c. onion, sliced
1/2 c. green pepper, chopped

2/3 c. barbecue sauce
2 T. Dijon mustard
2 c. red leaf lettuce, torn
2 c. green leaf lettuce, torn
Garnish: 1 tomato, sliced

Rinse pasta with cold water; drain well. Combine pasta, beef, onion and green pepper in a medium bowl; set aside. Mix together barbecue sauce and mustard in a small bowl; stir into beef mixture. Chill. At serving time, toss together red and green lettuce; arrange on salad plates. Spoon beef mixture over lettuce; garnish with tomato slices. Serves 4.

Curl a string of dried chile peppers into a circle,
then set a hurricane with a fat red candle in the center for a
quick and casual centerpiece.

Fridge Dinner Math

Meat		Veggies		Starch		Dressing		Add-Ins		Your Dinner
1/2 to 1 lb.	+	1-1/2 to 2 c.	+	2 c. cooked	+	1 to 1-1/2 c.	+	to taste	=	
canned tuna, drained	+	broccoli or cauliflower, chopped	+	elbow or shell macaroni	+	Italian salad dressing	+	fresh parsley, chervil, dill, chives; croutons	=	Tuna-Broccoli Macaroni Salad
chicken, cooked and diced	+	cucumber, sliced	+	potatoes, cubed	+	mayonnaise	+	yellow onions, red or green peppers, chopped; chow mein noodles	=	Chicken-Veggie Potato Salad
cheese, cubed or shredded	+	green or red peppers, sliced	+	rice, white or wild	+	mayonnaise-style salad dressing	+	pickle relish; French fried onions	=	Cheesy Rice Salad
4 to 5 eggs, hard-boiled, peeled and sliced	+	asparagus, cooked and sliced	+	couscous	+	plain yogurt	+	green olives, sliced; toasted almonds	=	Egg & Asparagus Couscous
bacon, crisply cooked and crumbled	+	cherry tomatoes, halved	+	rotini, penne or bowtie pasta	+	creamy blue cheese dressing	+	minced garlic; sunflower kernels	=	Bacon-Tomato Toss

Select meat, veggies (more than one, if you like), starch, dressing and add-ins from the table...read straight across or pick and choose. Combine in a large serving bowl. Mix well; chill. Serves 4.

Just Desserts

SWEET ENDINGS TO ONE-POT MEALS

Jenn's Pistachio-Cranberry Cookies

Debbie Button
Jarrettsville, MD

Last year my daughter Jenn and I were experimenting with some of our cookie recipes. She came up with this combination since the nuts, cranberries and chocolate chips were being used in other recipes. Voilà! Perfect for including in a cookie basket as an alternative to the traditional chocolate chip cookie.

18-1/2 oz. pkg. yellow cake mix
2 eggs, beaten
1/2 c. oil
1/2 c. pistachio nuts, chopped

1/2 c. sweetened dried
  cranberries
1/2 c. white chocolate chips

In a large bowl, combine dry cake mix, eggs and oil; mix well. Fold in nuts, cranberries and white chocolate chips. Drop by teaspoonfuls onto ungreased baking sheets. Bake at 350 degrees for 12 minutes, or until edges are lightly golden. Transfer cookies to a wire rack to cool. Makes about 3 dozen.

Nothing says "cozy home" like the aroma of fresh-baked cookies! Freeze individual balls of cookie dough...ready to bake at a moment's notice.

Chocolate Chip-Oatmeal Cookies

Terri Moore
Asheville, NC

Our favorite partner for a big glass of ice-cold milk.

3/4 c. shortening
1 c. brown sugar, packed
1/2 c. sugar
1 egg
1/4 c. water
1 t. vanilla extract
1 c. all-purpose flour

1 t. salt
1/2 t. baking soda
3 c. quick-cooking oats,
  uncooked
12-oz. pkg. semi-sweet
  chocolate chips

Blend shortening, sugars, egg, water and vanilla; add flour, salt and baking soda. Stir in oats and chocolate chips; drop by teaspoonfuls onto greased baking sheets. Bake at 350 degrees for 10 minutes. Makes 3 to 4 dozen.

Baking cookies is a great activity for first-time cooks. Even
the youngest children can help by dropping chocolate chips
into the mixing bowl or scooping out spoonfuls of dough.
Enjoying the baked cookies will encourage your little helpers
to learn more in the kitchen!

Just Desserts

Snickerdoodles

Tina Knotts
Cable, OH

I'll be sending care packages of this cookie to my daughter, Brittany, as she starts college this fall...it's her favorite!

1 c. margarine, softened
1-1/2 c. plus 3 T. sugar, divided
2 eggs
2-3/4 c. all-purpose flour

2 t. cream of tartar
1 t. baking soda
1/2 t. salt
2 t. cinnamon

Blend together margarine, 1-1/2 cups sugar and eggs; add flour, cream of tartar, baking soda and salt. Mix well; chill for one hour. Combine remaining sugar and cinnamon in a small bowl; set aside. Shape dough into balls; roll in sugar mixture. Arrange on ungreased baking sheets; bake at 400 degrees for 9 to 10 minutes. Let cool for 2 minutes before removing from baking sheets. Makes 3 to 4 dozen.

Pecan Cookie Balls

Jodi Eisenhooth
McVeytown, PA

Sweet, crisp little morsels to go with an after-dinner cup of tea or coffee.

1 c. butter, softened
4 T. powdered sugar
2 c. chopped pecans

1 T. vanilla extract
2 c. all-purpose flour
1 to 2 c. powdered sugar

Blend together butter and powdered sugar; add pecans, vanilla and flour. Wrap dough in plastic wrap; chill for about 3 hours. Form dough into 3/4-inch balls; place on ungreased baking sheets. Bake at 350 degrees for 10 minutes. Let cool; roll in powdered sugar. Makes 2-1/2 to 3 dozen.

No-Bake Fudge Cookies

Barbara Voight
Duluth, MN

These chewy, fudgy cookies are so easy to make.

1 c. butter
1 c. milk
4 c. sugar
1 t. salt
1 c. baking cocoa

2 c. chunky peanut butter
1 T. vanilla extract
4 c. quick-cooking oats,
   uncooked
2 c. flaked coconut

Combine butter, milk, sugar, salt and cocoa in a saucepan. Bring to a boil, stirring constantly for 2 minutes. Stir in peanut butter and vanilla; blend in oats and coconut. Drop by tablespoonfuls onto wax paper; cool until set. Makes 4 to 5 dozen.

Keep the cupboard stocked with a selection of colored jimmies, chocolate bits, chopped peanuts and even cookie crumbs for quick ice cream toppings.

Toffee Almond Treats

Chrissy Stanton
Odenton, MD

So easy to make...so tasty to eat!

1 sleeve saltine crackers
1 c. butter, melted
2 t. vanilla extract
1 c. sugar

12-oz. pkg. semi-sweet
   chocolate chips
1 c. sliced almonds

Line a baking sheet with aluminum foil; grease. Arrange crackers in a single layer on baking sheet; set aside. Stir together butter, vanilla and sugar in a saucepan; bring to a boil. Spread mixture over crackers; bake at 400 degrees for 4 to 5 minutes. Remove from heat; sprinkle with chocolate chips. Let stand until chips are melted; spread chips over sugar mixture. Sprinkle with almonds; chill for about 2 hours. Break into bite-size pieces. Makes about 2 dozen.

Honor a special someone on a special day with a plate kept just for the purpose. Use paint made for glass and china to write "You are Special Today" around the edge of a plate. Add simple designs like stars or flowers. Your "special day" plate will become a family tradition!

Easy 4-Layer Marshmallow Bars

Jessica Parker
Mulvane, KS

Spray a spatula with non-stick vegetable spray for ease in patting down sticky bar cookie ingredients.

18-1/2 oz. pkg. chocolate cake
   mix
1/4 c. butter, melted
1/4 c. water

3 c. mini marshmallows
1 c. candy-coated chocolates
1/2 c. peanuts, chopped

Combine cake mix, butter and water until blended; press in a greased 13"x9" baking pan. Bake at 375 degrees for 20 to 22 minutes. Layer marshmallows, chocolates and peanuts over the top. Return to oven for an additional 3 to 5 minutes or until marshmallows melt; let cool. Cut into bars. Makes 2 dozen.

Lazy Day Bars

Laura Parker
Evansville, IN

They'll think you went to a lot of effort...but you didn't!

18-1/2-oz. pkg. German
   chocolate cake mix
2 eggs
1/4 c. water

1/4 c. brown sugar, packed
1/4 c. butter, softened
1/2 c. chopped nuts
12-oz. pkg. chocolate chips

Blend together cake mix, eggs, water, sugar and butter; spread in a greased baking sheet. Sprinkle nuts and chips on top; bake at 350 degrees for 20 to 25 minutes. Cool for 10 minutes; cut into bars. Makes about 2 dozen.

A big clear glass canister is great for showing off a collection of cookie cutters on your countertop.

Cocoa Brownies

Mary Watkins
Mishawaka, IN

If you just can't wait, these brownies are delicious while they're still a little warm, straight from the pan.

1 c. sugar
2/3 c. all-purpose flour
1/2 c. baking cocoa
1/2 t. baking powder
1/2 c. margarine, melted

1 t. vanilla extract
2 eggs
3/4 c. semi-sweet chocolate
  chips

Combine sugar, flour, baking cocoa and baking powder; add margarine, vanilla and eggs. Spread in a greased 9"x9" baking pan; sprinkle with chocolate chips. Bake at 350 degrees for 20 to 25 minutes. Cut into squares. Makes 1-1/2 to 2 dozen.

Share laughs at Family Movie Night...bring out the home movies of when Mom & Dad were kids. Or share feature films that were extra-special to you when you were growing up. Pass the popcorn, please!

Double Crunch Bars

Jan Stafford
Chickamauga, GA

My friend, Debby, shared this recipe with me. Her 6 children and my 5 children all love these scrumptious bars!

4 c. quick-cooking oats, uncooked
1 c. brown sugar, packed
3/4 c. butter, melted
1/2 c. honey
1/2 c. flaked coconut

1/2 c. semi-sweet chocolate chips
1/2 c. chopped nuts
1 t. vanilla extract
1 t. cinnamon
1 t. salt

Mix all ingredients together; press into a greased jelly-roll pan. Bake at 450 degrees for 10 to 12 minutes or until golden; cool. Cut into bars. Makes about 2 dozen.

A muffin tin makes a sweet centerpiece...simply place a votive candle in each cup. Mix up candle colors for a festive look.

Just Desserts

Easy Lemon-Coconut Bars

Gail Putjenter
Norfolk, NE

Tart-sweet and easy as 1-2-3!

18-1/4 oz. pkg. angel food
    cake mix
2/3 c. flaked coconut

14-1/2 oz. can lemon pie filling
Garnish: powdered sugar

In a medium bowl, mix dry cake mix, coconut and pie filling just until blended. Pour into an ungreased jelly-roll pan. Bake at 350 degrees for 20 to 30 minutes or until center is firm. Sprinkle with powdered sugar; cut into squares. Makes about 1-1/2 dozen.

Luscious Lemon Bars

Pam Bendorf
Allen, TX

Enjoy these delicate bars with a steamy cup of tea.

2-3/4 c. all-purpose flour,
    divided
1 c. butter, softened
2-3/4 c. sugar, divided

4 eggs
1/2 c. lemon juice
1 t. baking powder
Garnish: powdered sugar

Mix 2 cups flour, butter and 3/4 cup sugar together until crumbly; press into the bottom of a lightly greased 13"x9" baking pan. Bake at 350 degrees for 15 minutes; let cool. In same bowl, beat eggs and lemon juice; slowly add remaining flour, sugar and baking powder. Pour over cooled crust; bake for an additional 25 minutes. Cool. Sprinkle with powdered sugar; cut into bars. Makes about 3 dozen.

A Grandma-style treat...roll out extra pie dough, cut into strips and sprinkle with cinnamon-sugar. Bake at 350 degrees until golden.

Apple Brownies

Jean Burgon
Riverhead, NY

These apple bar cookies are just right for tucking into a lunchbox.

1/2 c. butter
1 c. sugar
1 egg, beaten
1 c. plus 1 T. all-purpose flour
1 t. cinnamon

1/2 t. baking soda
1/2 t. baking powder
1/4 t. salt
1 c. apple, cored, peeled and
    chopped

Mix all ingredients together in order given in an ungreased
10"x10" baking pan. Bake at 350 degrees for 40 minutes. Cool and
cut into squares. Makes one dozen.

Watch for interesting plates at yard sales. They're just the
thing for delivering cookies to friends & neighbors...the
recipient will feel extra-special and the dish is theirs to keep.

Raspberry-Coconut Squares

Kathleen Jones
Hot Springs, AR

For a yummy change, try making these bar cookies with strawberry or apricot jam.

3/4 c. butter, softened
1 c. sugar
2 c. all-purpose flour
1-1/2 c. flaked coconut
1/2 c. chopped nuts

1 t. vanilla extract
1/4 t. salt
1 egg
16-oz. jar raspberry jam

Mix together all ingredients except jam; press three-quarters of mixture into a greased 13"x9" baking pan. Spread jam almost to the edges; drop remaining butter mixture by teaspoons over jam. Bake at 350 degrees for 35 to 40 minutes; cool and cut into squares. Makes about 3 dozen.

Homemade goodies being mailed to college students or faraway friends are a double treat when wrapped in familiar hometown newspapers.

Apricot Layer Bars

Marilyn Rogers
Point Townsend, WA

Stir in some chopped pecans for crunchiness.

1-3/4 c. quick-cooking oats,
   uncooked
1-3/4 c. all-purpose flour
1 c. brown sugar, packed

1 c. butter, softened
1/8 t. salt
12-oz. jar apricot preserves

Mix together oats, flour, brown sugar, butter and salt. Press half of mixture into a greased 8"x8" baking pan. Spread preserves over the top; top with remaining oat mixture. Bake at 350 degrees for 35 minutes. Let cool; cut into squares. Makes one to 1-1/2 dozen.

Need a quick snack for the kids? Make fruit pops! Blend together fresh or canned fruit with fruit juice and pour into ice cube trays or small paper cups. Insert wooden sticks before freezing.

Rhubarb Cream Cheesecake

Jenifer Bowser
Worthington, PA

This recipe is a hit wherever I take it!

1 c. plus 1 T. all-purpose flour,
    divided
1-1/4 c. sugar, divided
1/2 c. margarine, softened

3 c. rhubarb, cut in 1/2-inch
    pieces
12-oz. pkg. cream cheese
2 eggs, beaten

Mix together one cup flour, 1/4 cup sugar and margarine; press into a
10" pie plate. Set aside. Combine rhubarb, 1/2 cup sugar and
remaining flour. Toss lightly and pour into crust. Bake at 375 degrees
for 15 minutes. Beat together cream cheese, remaining sugar and
eggs until fluffy; pour over hot rhubarb mixture. Reduce oven to
350 degrees and bake for an additional 30 minutes or until set. Add
topping; cut into squares. Serves 6 to 8.

Topping:

8-oz. container sour cream
2 T. sugar

1 t. vanilla extract

Mix together all ingredients.

Look for a vintage
cookie jar at flea markets
or yard sales, then keep it
stocked with your
family's favorites. Sweet
memories in the making!

Peanut Butter Texas Sheet Cake

Kathi Rostash
Nevada, OH

*I made this for a church get-together and had
many requests for the recipe...so will you!*

2 c. all-purpose flour	1 c. water
2 c. sugar	1/4 c. creamy peanut butter
1/2 t. salt	2 eggs, beaten
1 t. baking soda	1 t. vanilla extract
1 c. butter	1/2 c. buttermilk

Sift together flour, sugar, salt and baking soda in a large bowl; set
aside. Combine butter, water and peanut butter in a saucepan over
medium heat; bring to a boil. Add to flour mixture and mix well; set
aside. Combine eggs, vanilla and buttermilk; add to peanut butter
mixture. Spread into a greased 15"x10" jelly-roll pan. Bake at
350 degrees for 15 to 20 minutes, until it springs back when gently
touched. Spread Peanut Butter Icing over warm cake. Makes 15 to
20 servings.

Peanut Butter Icing:

1/2 c. butter	16-oz. pkg. powdered sugar
1/4 c. creamy peanut butter	1 t. vanilla extract
1/3 c. plus 1 T. milk	

Combine butter, peanut butter and milk in a saucepan over medium
heat; bring to a boil. Remove from heat; stir in powdered sugar and
vanilla to a spreading consistency.

Just Desserts

Microwave Cherry Crisp Cobbler

*Jean Tillotson
Sanford, NC*

Serve warm, topped with vanilla ice cream...out of this world!

14-1/2 oz. can cherry pie filling
18-1/2 oz. pkg. white cake mix
2 T. brown sugar, packed

1 t. cinnamon
1/2 c. chopped pecans
1/2 c. margarine, melted

Spread cherry pie filling in an 8"x8" glass baking dish; set aside. Combine dry cake mix, brown sugar, cinnamon and pecans; mix well and sprinkle over pie filling. Drizzle with margarine; microwave on high for 13 minutes. Let stand for 5 minutes; cut into squares. Makes 8 servings.

Blueberry Crisp

*Laura Strausberger
Roswell, GA*

An old country favorite made easy with cake mix.

1 lb. blueberries
18-1/2 oz. pkg. spice cake mix,
    divided

1/2 c. butter, melted
1 c. flaked coconut
1 c. chopped nuts

Spread blueberries in an 8"x8" baking pan. Sprinkle with half the dry cake mix, reserving the remainder for another recipe. Sprinkle with butter, coconut and nuts. Bake at 350 degrees for 30 to 45 minutes or until golden and bubbly. Cut into squares. Serves 8.

A family in harmony will prosper in everything.
-Chinese proverb

Yummy Peach Dessert

Nina Roberts
Queensland, Australia

A tried & true sweet favorite that everyone loves.

1/2 c. all-purpose flour
1/2 t. baking soda
1/2 t. salt
1 c. sugar
1 egg, beaten

15-oz. can sliced peaches,
   drained and chopped
1/2 c. brown sugar, packed
1/4 c. chopped walnuts
Garnish: whipped cream

Sift together flour, baking soda and salt; add sugar. Stir in egg and peaches. Spread in a lightly greased 9"x9" baking dish. Sprinkle with brown sugar and walnuts. Bake at 350 degrees for one hour. Serve warm with whipped cream. Serves 12 to 14.

Make a homemade dessert extra-special with real whipped cream. Pour whipping cream into a chilled mixing bowl and beat on high speed with a hand mixer. When it begins to hold its shape, stir in sugar and vanilla extract to taste. Keep beating until soft peaks form. Mmm!

Just Desserts

Easy Apple Crisp

Nancy Willis
Farmington Hills, MI

Garnish with a dollop of whipped cream and a dusting of cinnamon.

4 c. apples, cored and sliced
1/2 c. brown sugar, packed
1/2 c. quick-cooking oats,
    uncooked

1/3 c. all-purpose flour
3/4 t. cinnamon
1/4 c. margarine

Arrange apple slices in a greased 11"x8" baking pan; set aside.
Combine remaining ingredients; stir until crumbly and sprinkle over
apples. Bake at 350 degrees for 30 to 35 minutes. Serves 12 to 14.

An old-fashioned tea ball makes a charming pull for your
kitchen window shade.

Apple-Cranberry Crisp

Brenda Derby
Northborough, MA

We like to make this using several different varieties of tart baking apples.

6 c. apples, peeled and sliced
3 c. cranberries
1 c. sugar
2 t. cinnamon
1 to 2 t. lemon juice

3/4 c. butter, sliced and divided
1 c. all-purpose flour
1 c. brown sugar, packed
Garnish: vanilla ice cream

Toss together apple slices, cranberries, sugar and cinnamon. Spread in a buttered 13"x9" glass baking dish. Sprinkle with lemon juice and dot with 1/4 cup butter. Blend remaining butter with flour and brown sugar until crumbly; sprinkle over apple mixture. Bake for one hour at 350 degrees. Serve warm with vanilla ice cream. Serves 10 to 12.

Turn a small pumpkin or winter squash into an unexpected floral centerpiece. Carefully cut a hole in the top and scoop out the insides. Set it on a dish, slip a water-filled tumbler inside and tuck in a bouquet of short-stemmed flowers.

Baked Caramel Apples

Jean Reiner
San Jose, CA

Warm, sweet and satisfying...a perfect dessert!

4 apples, cored, peeled and
   quartered
1 T. butter
1 T. all-purpose flour

1 c. brown sugar, packed
1 c. boiling water
1-1/2 c. mini marshmallows
1 t. vanilla extract

Arrange apples in a buttered 2-quart baking dish; set aside. Melt butter in a saucepan; blend in flour. Add sugar and water; heat until sugar dissolves. Stir in marshmallows until melted; bring to a boil. Pour mixture over apples. Bake at 350 degrees for 25 to 30 minutes, basting occasionally with sauce. Serves 4 to 6.

Microwave Bread Pudding

Sally Killian
Indianapolis, IN

A quick & easy version of this favorite comfort food.

2 T. butter
2 eggs
1 c. milk
1/3 c. sugar

1 t. vanilla extract
1/8 t. salt
2 c. bread, torn into one-inch
   pieces

Melt butter in a one-quart microwave-safe baking dish. Stir in eggs; blend well. Blend in milk, sugar, vanilla and salt. Stir in bread; mix until moistened. Let stand 5 minutes; microwave on high for 5-1/2 to 6 minutes. Serves 4 to 6.

Slow-Cooker Chocolate Pudding Cake
Tracie Smith
Bluffton, IN

Warm and chocolatey...yum!

18-1/4 oz. pkg. chocolate cake
    mix
3.9-oz. pkg. instant chocolate
    pudding mix
2 c. sour cream
4 eggs

1 c. water
3/4 c. oil
1 c. semi-sweet chocolate chips
Garnish: whipped cream or
    ice cream

Combine dry cake mix, pudding mix, sour cream, eggs, water and oil
in a mixing bowl. Blend on medium speed with a hand mixer for
2 minutes. Stir in chocolate chips. Pour into a slow cooker sprayed
with a non-stick vegetable spray. Cover and cook on low setting for
6 to 7 hours, until a toothpick comes out with moist crumbs. Serve
topped with whipped topping or ice cream. Makes 10 to 12 servings.

Slow-Cooker Caramel Apple Delight
Shelley Turner
Boise, ID

Serve this sweet, gooey delight over vanilla ice cream or
slices of angel food cake.

1/2 c. apple juice
7-oz. pkg. caramels, unwrapped
1 t. vanilla extract
1/2 t. cinnamon

1/3 c. creamy peanut butter
4 to 5 tart apples, cored, peeled,
    and sliced

Combine apple juice, caramels, vanilla and cinnamon in slow cooker.
Add peanut butter; mix well. Add apples; cover and cook on low
setting for 5 hours. Stir thoroughly, cover and cook on low setting
one additional hour. Makes 4 to 6 servings.

Mix-in-a-Pan Nut Cake

Phyllis Peters
Three Rivers, MI

So simple to stir up...just right with a pot of coffee and a good friend.

1/2 c. margarine
6-oz. jar strained carrot baby food
1 c. crushed pineapple with juice
1 egg, beaten
1 c. sugar

1-1/4 c. all-purpose flour
1 t. baking soda
2 t. cinnamon
1 t. vanilla extract
1 c. chopped English walnuts

Melt margarine in a 9"x9" baking pan. Gradually add remaining ingredients to pan; blend well. Bake at 325 degrees for 35 to 40 minutes. Serves 8 to 10.

A teddy bear tea party...set a low table with a lacy tablecloth, a nosegay of sweet flowers and your best teacups. Add a pot of herbal tea, little sandwiches cut in fancy shapes and a big platter of dainty cookies. Don't forget honey for the bears!

Old-Fashioned Applesauce Cake

Gail Hageman
Albion, ME

Applesauce makes the cake moist and tender.

2 c. sugar
1/2 c. shortening
2 eggs
1/2 c. water
1-1/2 c. applesauce
2-1/2 c. all-purpose flour
1-1/2 t. baking soda

1/4 t. baking powder
1-1/2 t. salt
3/4 t. cinnamon
1/2 t. ground cloves
1/2 t. allspice
1/2 c. chopped walnuts

Blend together sugar and shortening; beat in eggs, water and applesauce. Gradually add flour, baking soda, baking powder, salt and spices. Mix thoroughly; stir in nuts. Pour into a greased, floured 13"x9" baking pan. Bake at 350 degrees for one hour or until cake tests done; watch that edges don't get too dark. Makes 8 to 10 servings.

A fragrant cup of cinnamon coffee is the perfect partner for Old-Fashioned Applesauce Cake. Just add a teaspoon of cinnamon and 1/4 cup of brown sugar to the coffeepot before brewing.

Cherry-Pineapple Dump Cake

Donna Jo Brown
Peru, IL

Nothing beats this recipe...simply dump in the ingredients, one after another! This cake is a "must" at all Brown family functions.

14-1/2 oz. can cherry pie filling
20-oz. can chunk pineapple,
   drained and 1/2 of juice
   reserved

18-1/2 oz. pkg. yellow cake mix
1 t. vanilla extract
1 c. butter, melted
1 c. chopped pecans

Spread pie filling in a greased and floured 13"x9" baking pan; top with pineapple and reserved juice. Stir in dry cake mix and vanilla. Drizzle butter over top; sprinkle with pecans. Bake at 350 degrees for 40 to 45 minutes or until golden. Serves 8 to 10.

Orange-Peach Dump Cake

Elizabeth Wenk
Cuyahoga Falls, OH

A different flavor combination for this trusty dessert.

14-1/2 oz. can peach pie filling,
   chopped
18-oz. pkg. orange cake mix

2 eggs
1/2 c. sour cream

Combine all ingredients in an ungreased 13"x9" baking pan. Mix with a fork until well blended; smooth top. Bake at 350 degrees for 40 to 45 minutes. Serves 8 to 10.

Crustless Pumpkin Pie ▶

Linda Webb
Delaware, OH

*My favorite pumpkin dessert...too good to save
only for Thanksgiving!*

4 eggs, beaten
15-oz. can pumpkin
12-oz. can evaporated milk
1-1/2 c. sugar
2 t. pumpkin pie spice
1 t. salt

18-1/2 oz. pkg. yellow cake mix
1 c. chopped pecans or walnuts
1 c. butter, melted
Optional: whipped topping,
    chopped nuts, cinnamon

Combine eggs, pumpkin, evaporated milk, sugar, spice and salt. Mix well; pour into an ungreased 13"x9" baking pan. Sprinkle dry cake mix and nuts over top. Drizzle with butter; do not stir. Bake at 350 degrees for 45 minutes to one hour, testing for doneness with a toothpick. Serve with whipped topping, sprinkled with nuts and cinnamon. Makes 8 to 10 servings.

Pumpkin Cake

Darlene Hartzler
Marshallville, OH

*My grandma used to make this cake all the time when we were kids.
We love it with a little whipped topping.*

15-oz. can pumpkin
1 c. oil
4 eggs
2 c. all-purpose flour
2 c. sugar

1 c. chopped walnuts
2 t. baking soda
2 t. baking powder
2 t. cinnamon
1/2 t. salt

Combine all ingredients; blend well. Pour into a greased 13"x9" baking pan. Bake at 350 degrees for 45 minutes. Serves 8 to 10.

Eclair Cake ▶

Cheryl Frost
Woodstock, OH

Luscious cream filling and chocolatey topping...best with a tall, cold glass of milk!

1 c. water
1/2 c. butter
1 c. all-purpose flour
4 eggs, beaten
8-oz. pkg. cream cheese,
    softened

3 c. milk
2 3-oz. pkgs. instant vanilla
    pudding mix
8-oz. container frozen whipped
    topping, thawed
Garnish: chocolate syrup

Combine water and butter in a saucepan; heat until boiling. Whisk in flour until smooth; remove from heat. Pour mixture into a medium bowl; gradually blend in eggs. Spread in a greased 13"x9" baking pan; bake at 350 degrees for 30 minutes. Remove from oven; press baked crust down lightly and set aside. With an electric mixer on medium speed, beat together cream cheese, milk and pudding mix for 2 minutes; spread over crust. Refrigerate until firm. At serving time, spread with whipped topping; drizzle with chocolate syrup. Serves 12 to 15.

WELCOME

Welcome your guests with an inviting door mat. Select a plain grass mat and stencil "Welcome" or "Home Sweet Home" on it with acrylic paints. When the paint dries, spray with clear acrylic sealer.

Banana Split Cake

Pat Mollohan
Parkersburg, WV

My family loves this cake...it never lasts more than a day! You can use 2 layer cakes instead of the angel food cake, if you like.

1 angel food cake
16-oz. container frozen whipped topping, thawed
3 to 4 bananas, sliced
6-oz. jar maraschino cherries, drained and sliced
4-oz. can crushed pineapple, drained
1/2 c. chopped nuts, divided
Garnish: chocolate syrup, caramel syrup

Cut cake in half horizontally; set the top half aside. Place bottom half on a cake plate; spread with a layer of whipped topping. Arrange banana slices and cherries on whipped topping; spread pineapple over bananas. Sprinkle with 1/4 cup nuts; set aside. Spread the bottom of remaining cake with whipped topping; set on top of bottom half. Spread remaining whipped topping over the entire cake. Drizzle cake with chocolate and caramel syrups; sprinkle with remaining nuts. Chill for one hour before serving. Serves 8 to 10.

The ordinary arts we practice every day at home
are of more importance to the soul than
their simplicity might suggest.
-Thomas More

Just Desserts

Fabulous Light Key Lime Pie

Jan Sofranko
Malta, IL

So delicious you won't believe it's low-fat.

1/3 c. Key lime juice
14-oz. can light sweetened
   condensed milk
3 to 5 drops green food coloring
8-oz. container low-fat frozen
   whipped topping, thawed

9-inch low-fat graham
   cracker crust
Optional: 1 lime, thinly sliced

Mix lime juice with condensed milk in a large bowl. Blend in food coloring until lightly tinted. Carefully fold in whipped topping. Spoon into pie crust; garnish with slices of lime, if desired. Refrigerate for several hours or overnight. Serves 6 to 8.

Sour Cream Lemon Pie

Kelli Nielsen
Orovada, NV

A tart, creamy ending to your meal.

1 c. sugar
3-1/2 T. cornstarch
1 T. lemon zest
1/2 c. lemon juice
3 egg yolks, beaten
1 c. milk

1/4 c. butter
1 c. sour cream
9-inch pie crust, baked
1 c. whipping cream, whipped
Garnish: twists of lemon zest

Combine sugar, cornstarch, lemon zest, lemon juice, egg yolks and milk in a saucepan. Cook over medium heat for 3 to 5 minutes until thickened. Stir in butter; cool to room temperature. Stir in sour cream; spoon into pie crust. Cover with whipped cream; garnish with lemon twists. Chill before serving. Serves 6 to 8.

Sweet Hummingbird Cake

Wendy Lee Paffenroth
Pine Island, NY

*A sprinkle of chopped pecans makes a nice finish
to this rich cake.*

8-oz. can crushed pineapple
2 to 3 bananas, sliced
1/2 c. milk
2 eggs
1/4 c. oil

1 t. vanilla extract
Optional: 1/4 c. dark rum
18-1/2 oz. pkg. banana
   cake mix
16-oz. can vanilla frosting

Beat together pineapple with juice, bananas, milk, eggs, oil, vanilla extract and rum, if using, until well blended. Stir in cake mix until moistened. Pour into a greased and floured Bundt® cake pan. Bake at 350 degrees on middle oven rack for 40 minutes, until top springs back when touched. Cool for at least 45 minutes; invert onto a serving plate. Microwave frosting on high setting 15 to 20 seconds, until runny. Let stand for a minute before drizzling over cake. Serves 12.

For easy-to-make frosting that's not too sweet,
simply blend together a 16-ounce can of frosting with an
8-ounce package of softened cream cheese.

Just Desserts

Perfect Arkansas Apple Pie

Susan Young
Wolcottville, IN

Back in 1968, I was living in a small town in Arkansas where my husband was going to college. I made many friends there. When we left, a dear friend organized a going-away party and a huge cookbook of friends' favorite recipes. This special recipe was hers.

6 c. Granny Smith apples,
   peeled, cored and thinly
   sliced
3/4 c. plus 1 t. sugar, divided
1/4 t. salt
1 t. cinnamon

1/8 t. nutmeg
2 T. all-purpose flour
2 T. lemon juice
2 9-inch pie crusts
2 T. butter, diced
1 t. milk

In a large mixing bowl, combine apples, 3/4 cup sugar, salt, cinnamon, nutmeg, flour and lemon juice. Place one pie crust in a 9" pie plate; spoon filling into crust and dot with butter. Top with remaining crust; crimp and seal edges. Make 4 cuts near center to vent. Brush with milk and sprinkle with remaining sugar. Bake at 425 degrees for 45 minutes. Serves 8.

If you have extra pie from the day before, treat yourself
to warm pie à la mode…mmm! Top a slice with a scoop
of ice cream, then microwave on high for just 10 to
15 seconds. The pie will be just-from-the-oven warm,
and the ice cream will stay firm.

Dana's Pecan Pie

Dana Warren
Hodgenville, KY

Can anything be better than a pecan pie? Yes...2 pecan pies!

2 9-inch pie crusts
4 eggs, beaten
1 c. sugar
1-1/2 c. dark corn syrup

1 t. vanilla extract
2 c. chopped pecans, divided
1/4 c. all-purpose flour

Place crusts in two, 9" pie plates; set aside. Blend together eggs, sugar, corn syrup, vanilla and one cup pecans. Stir in flour and remaining pecans. Divide mixture evenly between pie crusts; bake at 375 degrees for 30 to 45 minutes or until centers are set but soft. Makes 2 pies; each serves 6 to 8.

Trish's Peanut Butter Pie

Trish Gothard
Greenville, KY

Make it extra peanutty...sprinkle with chopped peanuts.

1/2 c. creamy peanut butter
1/2 c. milk
1/2 c. cream cheese, softened
8-oz. container frozen whipped
    topping, thawed

9-inch graham cracker crumb
    pie crust

Combine peanut butter, milk and cream cheese in a bowl; blend until smooth. Fold in whipped topping; pour into pie crust. Freeze for about 30 minutes; store in the refrigerator. Serves 6 to 8.

Fruit Salad & Honey-Yogurt Dressing
Kathy Unruh
Fresno, CA

This tropical delight is just the ticket on a hot summer day.

1 pt. strawberries, hulled and quartered
1 pt. blueberries
1 cantaloupe, peeled and cubed
1 pineapple, peeled and cubed
2 mangoes, peeled and cubed
2 papayas, peeled and cubed
1/2 c. sliced toasted almonds

Combine all ingredients together in a large serving bowl. Toss with dressing; chill. Makes 6 to 8 servings.

Dressing:

1-1/2 c. plain yogurt
1/4 c. powdered sugar
1/3 c. honey
1/8 t. almond extract
1/2 t. ground ginger
1/2 t. allspice
1/8 t. cinnamon
1 t. fresh mint, chopped

Combine all ingredients; mix well.

Turn a wooden birdhouse from the craft store into a sweet tissue holder. Carefully pull the roof loose and reattach it on one side with 2 small hinges. Paint the birdhouse, then slip a tissue box inside and pull tissues through the hole in front.

Refreshing Frozen Fruit Salad

Janette Diem
Shippensburg, PA

I like to serve this simple salad with cake or cookies. It takes the place of ice cream very well!

8-oz. pkg. cream cheese,
   softened
3/4 c. sugar
8-oz. container frozen whipped
   topping, thawed
3 bananas, sliced

16-oz. pkg. strawberries, hulled
   and quartered
20-oz. can crushed pineapple,
   drained
1 c. chopped nuts

Blend cream cheese, sugar and whipped topping together in a freezer-safe bowl; fold in fruits and nuts. Freeze. Let stand for 15 to 20 minutes at room temperature before serving. Serves 12 to 15.

It's simple to give new wooden benches or planting boxes
a weathered, rustic appearance. Use a stiff wire brush to
brush wood along the grain, then apply a dark or gray stain.
With a cloth, wipe away extra stain while it's still wet.
Once the stain dries, apply a wood sealer to preserve the
newly weathered wood.

• Just Desserts •

Sweet Ambrosia Salad ▶️

Rachel Ripley
Pittsburgh, PA

Kids of all ages love this sweet, creamy salad!

20-oz. can pineapple chunks,
    drained
14-1/2 oz. jar maraschino
    cherries, drained
11-oz. can mandarin oranges,
    drained

8-oz. container sour cream
10-1/2 oz. pkg. pastel mini
    marshmallows
1/2 c. sweetened flaked
coconut

Combine fruit in a large bowl; stir in sour cream until coated. Fold in marshmallows and coconut; cover and chill overnight. Makes 8 to 10 servings.

Tea-dye a white tablecloth for a warm country look. Fill a large pot with water, bring to a boil and steep 8 or 10 teabags. Prewash tablecloth, then add to pot and simmer for at least 30 minutes, until it's as dark as you like. Rinse and dry.

Winter Fruit in Vanilla Syrup

Kasie Keeling
Saint Louis, MO

This blend of dried fruits is especially good with roast meats.

1-1/2 c. water
1-1/2 c. sugar
1/8 t. salt
2 T. vanilla extract
1 t. lemon juice
1/2 t. cinnamon

1/2 c. dried apricots
1/2 c. dried cranberries
1/2 c. dried plums
1/2 c. dried figs
3 pears, cored, peeled and sliced
3 T. butter

In a saucepan, heat water, sugar and salt until dissolved. Bring to a boil; reduce heat and simmer for 10 minutes. Stir in vanilla, lemon juice and cinnamon. Add apricots, cranberries, plums, figs and pears; simmer for 20 to 30 minutes. Cool to room temperature; cover and refrigerate overnight. At serving time, bring to a simmer; stir in butter. Let cool slightly and serve. Makes 8 to 10 servings.

A large vintage canning jar filled with Winter Fruit in Vanilla Syrup makes a thoughtful hostess gift. Tie on a topper of colorful fabric with raffia.

S'more Bars

Jo Ann

All the campfire flavor of s'mores...enjoy them anytime!

8 to 10 whole graham crackers
20-oz. pkg. brownie mix
2 c. mini marshmallows

1 c. semi-sweet chocolate chips
2/3 c. chopped pecans

Arrange graham crackers in a single layer in a greased 13"x9" baking pan; set aside. Prepare brownie mix according to package directions; spread carefully over graham crackers. Bake at 350 degrees for 25 to 30 minutes. Sprinkle marshmallows, chocolate chips and pecans over brownie layer; bake for an additional 5 minutes or until golden. Cut into bars when cool. Makes 2 dozen.

Grilled Banana Boats

Nancy Molldrem
Eau Claire, WI

Kids love these...a fun summertime dessert!

4 bananas
6-oz. pkg. semi-sweet chocolate
    chips

10-1/2 oz. pkg. mini
    marshmallows

Pull back one section of peel on each banana; do not remove. Cut a wedge-shaped section out of each banana; fill with chocolate chips and marshmallows. Replace peels; wrap each banana in foil. Heat on grill about 6 minutes, until chips and marshmallows are melted, or bake at 350 degrees for 7 to 10 minutes. Makes 4 servings.

Dessert Math

Whip up a tasty ending to any meal with foods you keep on hand. So easy yet looks so festive!

Base		Fruit		Sprinkles		Your Dessert
2 c.	+	1 c.	+	1/2 to 1 c.	=	
vanilla ice cream	+	cherry pie filling	+	chocolate sandwich cookies, crumbled	=	Cherry-Cookie Swirl
chocolate pudding	+	strawberries, sliced	+	mini chocolate chips	=	Chocolate-Strawberry Parfait
lemon yogurt	+	mandarin oranges, drained	+	chopped nuts	=	Special Citrus Dessert
orange sherbet	+	crushed pineapple, drained	+	pound cake, cubed	=	Tropical Delight
strawberry gelatin, cubed	+	bananas, sliced	+	toasted coconut	=	Strawberry-Coconut Parfait

Start by scooping the dessert base into pretty dessert dishes or parfait glasses. Alternate with layers of fruit plus some thawed frozen whipped topping, if you like. Top off with sprinkles of your choice. Serves 4. Yummy!

Use this handy formula to stir up quick meals with what you have on hand. Just copy, cut and hang on the fridge or inside a cabinet door for easy reference!

·INDEX·

·INDEX·

· I N D E X ·

Send us your favorite recipe!

and the memory that makes it special for you! If we select your recipe for a brand-new **Gooseberry Patch** cookbook, your name will appear right along with it...and you'll receive a FREE copy of the book.

Share your recipe on our website at
www.gooseberrypatch.com

Or mail to:

Gooseberry Patch • Attn: Cookbook Dept.
2500 Farmers Dr., #110 • Columbus, OH 43235

*Don't forget to include your name, address, phone number and email address so we'll know how to reach you for your FREE book!

Since 1992, we've been publishing country cookbooks for every kitchen and for every meal of the day! Each has hundreds of budget-friendly recipes, using ingredients you already have on hand. Their lay-flat binding makes them easy to use and each is filled with hand-drawn artwork and plenty of personality.

Have a taste for more?

Call us toll-free at
1•800•854•6673

Find us here too!

We created our official **Circle of Friends** so we could fill everyone in on the latest scoop at once. Visit us online to join in the fun and discover free recipes, exclusive giveaways and much more!

www.gooseberrypatch.com

U.S. to Metric Recipe Equivalents

Volume Measurements

1/4 teaspoon	1 mL
1/2 teaspoon	2 mL
1 teaspoon	5 mL
1 tablespoon = 3 teaspoons	15 mL
2 tablespoons = 1 fluid ounce	30 mL
1/4 cup	60 mL
1/3 cup	75 mL
1/2 cup = 4 fluid ounces	125 mL
1 cup = 8 fluid ounces	250 mL
2 cups = 1 pint =16 fluid ounces	500 mL
4 cups = 1 quart	1 L

Weights

1 ounce	30 g
4 ounces	120 g
8 ounces	225 g
16 ounces = 1 pound	450 g

Oven Temperatures

300° F	150° C
325° F	160° C
350° F	180° C
375° F	190° C
400° F	200° C
450° F	230° C

Baking Pan Sizes

Square

8x8x2 inches	2 L = 20x20x5 cm
9x9x2 inches	2.5 L = 23x23x5 cm

Rectangular

13x9x2 inches	3.5 L = 33x23x5 cm

Loaf

9x5x3 inches	2 L = 23x13x7 cm

Round

8x1-1/2 inches	1.2 L = 20x4 cm
9x1-1/2 inches	1.5 L = 23x4 cm